Journey to Koinonia

An Interracial

Small Group Experience

Terry Roberts, D.Min.

The Companion Guide to
Beyond Reconciliation:
Experiencing Koinonia Across the Racial Divide

ISBN: 979-8-6380-9314-3

DEDICATION

This book is lovingly dedicated to the fourteen individuals—all of them members of Trinity Church—who "traveled" with me on our very first "Journey to *Koinonia*." Their faithful participation and interaction contributed greatly to the success of the "Journey" and validated the concepts contained in this book.

I would also like to thank the congregation of Trinity Church for loving me through this period of my life, when I was doing the research and writing my conclusions, much of which made its way into my Sunday morning sermons. Thank you for your willingness to learn with me and for your patience with me when at times I may have been a little over-zealous in my excitement about the things I was learning.

My wife, Sandra, has been a constant source of encouragement and support for this project. She was by my side throughout the Journey to *Koinonia,* serving the group at every turn. She has continued to encourage me and support me as we endeavor to live out the principles in this book.

CONTENTS

Acknowledgments i

Introduction 3

1 The Journey Story 7

2 The Meetings: A Closer Look 21

3 Results of the Journey 33

4 Facilitator's Guide 41

Conclusion 91

About the Author 93

Other Books by the Author 95

ACKNOWLEDGMENTS

This book is the product of many hours of research, writing, and a six-week-long field study in a local church. More than that, it is the result of much prayer, consultation, and assistance from many people, including those I mentioned on the dedication page.

Additionally, I would like to thank my professors at the Assemblies of God Theological Seminary for their encouragement and help with this project. Among them are Dr. Wayne Lee, director of my Doctor of Ministry cohort, and Dr. Lois Olena, my project director. Without their insights and encouragement, this book and its companion, *Beyond Reconciliation: Experiencing Koinonia Across the Racial Divide*, would not exist.

Finally, to Jesus, my Lord and faithful Friend, who is teaching me to love everyone He loves.

Introduction

This book is a companion to my larger work, *Beyond Reconciliation: Experiencing Koinonia across the Racial Divide.* In that book I sought to make the case that racial reconciliation—wonderful as it is—is not enough. Something more is needed. Reconciliation involves forgiveness and a willingness to accept people we formerly avoided, and those are essential biblical values, to be sure. But we need more. We need interracial *Koinonia.* (*Koinonia* is a word from the Greek New Testament, often translated "fellowship.")

My book *Beyond Reconciliation* defines biblical *koinonia,* describes what it looks like in actual practice, and shares the immense benefits to those who experience it. Here's an example of those benefits, which I quote from another author:

> "When we take time to be with people, a relationship is developed. Both parties drop their masks; they respect each other's convictions and understand each other's sufferings. … As we listen to our friend's real beliefs and problems, we divest our minds of the false images we may have harbored, and we are determined also to be real. … We no longer desire to score points or win a victory. We love the person too much to boost our ego at his or her expense."[1]

---

[1] Michael Pocock and Joseph Henriques, *Cultural Change and Your Church: Helping Your Church Thrive in a Diverse Society* (Grand Rapids, MI: Baker Books, 2002), 158.

In my book *Beyond Reconciliation*, I also explain why *koinonia* comes only with intentionality, courage, and determination: When believers from different races come together in one congregation, even if they agree on doctrine and moral values, they often disagree stridently about other things, such as politics. For example, white Evangelicals often champion moral righteousness causes, such as the sanctity of human life and marriage—and therefore tend to vote Republican. On the other hand, Black Christians, who poll more conservatively on moral values than their white counterparts, also care deeply about social justice issues like poverty and equal access—and therefore, tend to vote Democratic. These polarizing loyalties, often laced with deep emotion, can cause a racial-political divide that author Alice Patterson calls the "Grand Canyon" of division in the Church.[2]

Beyond Reconciliation honestly explores that "canyon," with a view to building bridges of understanding across the divide. This book you are now holding outlines one of those bridges—a simple strategy that facilitates *koinonia* across the racial-political divide. That strategy is a six-week, small-group experience I conducted with fourteen members of Trinity Church, where I serve as Lead Pastor. Half of the participants were white and the other half were black. We called the experience "Journey to *Koinonia.*"

This book tells all about that experience, and for those who want to conduct their own "journey," it includes a Facilitator's Guide that will walk you through the process. Here's a summary of the book's contents:

- In Chapter one, I tell the story of what led to our first "Journey," and I share a simple overview of the six-week experience—how I planned and implemented it, selected and recruited participants, and evaluated its results.

---

[2] Alice Patterson, *Bridging the Racial and Political Divide*

- In Chapter Two, I drill deeper into each of the weekly meetings, sharing lots of details about the various activities and topics.
- Chapter Three presents the results of the journey and describes the instruments I used to measure those results.
- Chapter Four is the Facilitator's Guide with step-by-step instructions and copies of all the materials used in the Journey.

If you have not already read my book *Beyond Reconciliation: Experiencing Koinonia across the Racial Divide*, I recommend that you get a copy and keep it as a companion to this book. Of course, if you decide to conduct a Journey to *Koinonia*, you will want to use *Beyond Reconciliation* as your basic curriculum.

1

THE JOURNEY STORY

During my doctoral studies, I was asked to select a topic for my dissertation. (Actually, it was called a "project," because it involved several phases: research, writing, and a field study or implementation). As I prayerfully pondered various ideas, I settled on the topic of race relations in the local church.

As pastor of a multi-racial church, I had experienced the richness and beauty that comes with an ethnically diverse congregation. I also noticed that, beyond our worship services, our people didn't seem to engage in a lot of fellowship across racial lines. They got along well together at church, worshiped and prayed well together, seemed to enjoy the same sermons and even the same music. But when the worship service ended, everyone went to their own homes or restaurants and didn't meet again until the next Sunday. As I like to phrase it, our people worshipped together on Sunday, but they didn't eat together on Monday.

In my book *Beyond Reconciliation*, I share the following experience which illustrates my point:

> A few years ago, I took a couple dozen of our church members to a state-wide church conference. At noon, when the participants broke for lunch, I went looking for our people in the cafeteria. The arrangement was open seating, and I wanted to sit with our folks. What I found surprised and disappointed me. Our white members

were seated together at one table and our black members at another table nearby. I walked over to the tables, got their attention, and asked, "What is this? Are we back to the days of segregation?" My question evoked nervous laughter, but no one answered. I think they were a bit embarrassed. Good. I wanted to make the point that their seating arrangement was *not* good. I think they got the point.[3]

As a student of Scripture, I knew instinctively that something was wrong with that picture. I knew that the New Testament frequently exhorts God's people about their relationships with each other—what we often refer to as the "one another" scriptures. If you've never done this, look in your concordance (or do a computer search) for the words "one another" (or "each other" in some translations), and you will be surprised at the sheer volume of verses that address our interpersonal relationships in the body of Christ.

One of those verses—Romans 15:7—exhorts believers to "accept one another." This exhortation is given to believers who lived in a cross-cultural context. The word "accept" (rendered "welcome" in some translations) means more than just "be okay with or" or "be nice to." Within this context, it means to intentionally reach out to believers of a different culture than your own, and bring them into your fellowship![4]

I also understood a bit about the wonderful word *koinonia*—the New Testament Greek word for fellowship.[5] As I compared what I knew of that word with what I saw happening (or not happening) in our congregation, I realized something needed to change. That something would be the subject of my dissertation. I decided to research the whole area of race relations within a local church, and on the basis of

---

[3] Terry Roberts, *Beyond Reconciliation: Experiencing Koinonia Across the Racial Divide*, p. 8.

[4] For an extensive study of this word, see Chapter 10 of *Beyond Reconciliation*.

[5] For an extensive study of this word, see Chapter 9 of *Beyond Reconciliation*.

that research, to design an intervention that would facilitate biblical fellowship—*koinonia*—across racial lines. That intervention took shape as the six-week, small group experience called "Journey to *Koinonia*."

The benefits of the small group format were already a given in my mind. I had seen and experienced the power of a few believers gathering face-to-face to eat together, laugh, pray, and share their burdens with each other—in short, "to do life together."

What I didn't know was whether a small group experience could also be used to strengthen relationships across racial lines. If so, what would that look like? What would the meetings consist of? Would it be good enough to just get people together and let nature take its course? Or, should the meeting include components designed intentionally to address the issues of race, culture, history, and politics—all the things that tend to divide us, or at least inject tension into our relationships?

My research answered those questions. As I explored the wealth of information on the topic, both in the biblical-theological genre and the contemporary literature, I came to a number of conclusions that shaped the final product called "Journey to Koinonia." Here are some of those conclusions:

1) The Church is a new kind of community on earth, commissioned to display God's inclusive love for all humanity and to gather a multi-ethnic body of believers for His glory. The highly descriptive word "manifold," used only once in Scripture, is applied to the wisdom of God on display in the Church. The word literally means "many-many-colored."

2) Ethnic diversity brings not only cultural richness, but also spiritual vitality to a local church and, in light of the "browning of America," ethnic diversity enhances a church's outreach potential. Furthermore, studies show that racial integration in a church setting does more to improve race relations than in any other social setting.

3) Sadly, only seven percent of churches in America are multi-ethnic. The good news: That statistic is changing. From 1998 to 2007 (less than 10 years), the percentage of Evangelical mega-churches that are multi-ethnic has risen from 6 to 25 percent.

4) Assuming their church is situated in a diverse community, Pastors can grow a multi-ethnic congregation by teaching on the beauty and power of diversity and then modeling diversity in their staffing and lay leaders, and in their own social interaction.

5) *Koinonia*-based unity, centered in Jesus and empowered by the Holy Spirit, serves as a potent adhesive that holds believers together despite their differences, and through them, displays to a divided world the manifold wisdom of God.

6) Multi-ethnic churches can experience inter-racial *koinonia* through small group encounters conducted in a spiritual and relational atmosphere that includes instruction, fellowship, and candid dialogue.

These conclusions shaped the nature and content of the Journey. In fact, the last few words of point 6 state the essential components of the small group meetings: "a spiritual and relational atmosphere that includes instruction, fellowship, and candid dialogue."

The balance of this chapter is an overview of how we incorporated those components into our Journey experience.

Weekly Meetings

The six weekly meetings on our Journey provided opportunities for the participants to: 1) hear teaching on a series of relevant topics, 2) share and listen to one another in guided dialogue sessions, so as to better understand each other's life journey, 3) experience interracial *koinonia* through the spiritual and relational atmosphere of the meetings, 4) express repentance and forgiveness, and 5) become a model for future multi-ethnic small group experiences.

Preparation

Before the Journey could begin, a series of preparatory steps were necessary. These steps included recruiting participants, planning the meetings, writing the curriculum, and creating instruments to measure outcomes.

Selecting and Recruiting Participants

A few concerns guided the selection of participants: First, I wanted the group evenly divided along racial lines. Second, I sought variety in age and gender. I intentionally chose a few older people who could recall the days of Jim Crow. On the younger end of the spectrum, I wanted a certain measure of maturity—people with sufficient life experience to inform their contribution to the group and responsible enough to fulfill expectations.

Journey Participants by Race, Age, and Gender

Black	Age		White	Age
Female	31		Female	32
Female	32		Male	38
Male	56		Female	39
Female	57		Male	41
Female	63		Female	57
Male	64		Male	57
Female	71		Female	76

Due to the potential volatility of some of the topics, I looked for people with the capacity to demonstrate respect for others. I also chose participants at varying stages in their spiritual walk and in their understanding of race relations. Those who ultimately accepted my invitation included seven Blacks and seven Whites, for a total of fourteen participants. Including my wife and me, the group totaled sixteen. However, due to occasional absences, the six meetings averaged fourteen in attendance.

The participants represented a range of political ideologies. We administered an anonymous questionnaire with five political options, which yielded somewhat surprising results (see Table below).[6] Remarkably, two Blacks indicated they were "conservative," and the only "liberal" in the group was white. One black participant selected "other" and specified, "All the above, depending on the issue." I used the terms "liberal" and "conservative" on the questionnaire to ascertain whether participants tend to vote Democratic or Republican. However, in retrospect, the labels "conservative" and "liberal" appear inadequate and potentially misleading, because the same individual can hold liberal sentiments about certain issues and conservative leanings about others. Instead of using these labels, I suggest you simply ask the participants to identify which political party they usually vote for (see the pre-Journey Questionnaire in Section Four).

Journey Participants by Political Ideology

Ideology	*Black*	*White*
Conservative	2	5
Liberal		1
Moderate		1
Prefer not to say	4	
Other(please specify)	1 ("All the above, depending on the issue.")	

Finally, the participants represented the following vocations: one educator, one retail manager, one graphic artist, one self-employed, one retired teacher, two government service employees, three clerical workers, and one homemaker. One participant receives disability retirement, and another is in the process of applying for disability.

---

[6] See Section Four for the pre-journey and post-journey questionnaires.

Planning the Meetings and Pre-Session Reading

In order to maximize impact, the meetings would require a number of components. First, they should begin on a spiritual note, with a few minutes of worship and prayer. In order to honor the diverse musical tastes among the participants, I would ask them to take turns choosing and leading a song to open each meeting. This proved as simple as a sing-a-long using recorded music. Second, since each meeting revolves around a particular topic reflected in teaching and dialogue, I had to write the curriculum and prepare dialogue questions for the meetings. (That curriculum is contained in my book *Beyond Reconciliation: Experiencing Koinonia Across the Racial Divide.*)

Because of the importance of honest dialogue, I devised rules of engagement to guide this process. These "rules" included a concept known as "talking to the campfire," which allows participants to share their thoughts in a non-threatening way.[7] I cannot overstate the importance of dialogue to interracial *koinonia.*

Third, a time of fellowship over food would provide informal interaction among the participants and potentially reduce the intensity of the encounter. I decided to ask participants to volunteer to bring the food.

As a location for the meetings, I chose our church campus, particularly, a small, multi-purpose chapel in which we could arrange chairs as needed and set up refreshments. Since the day and time of the meetings must fit the participants' schedules, I decided to give them a say in that matter—something determined in the orientation meeting. Because several of the participants had small children, I arranged childcare for each of the meetings, with our church bearing the expense.

---

[7] I borrowed this concept from Edgar H. Schein (*Organizational Culture and Leadership*, 391-92), and I explain it in more detail in "Dialogue Rules of Engagement" in Section Four.

Curriculum and Dialogue Questions

My preparation for our first Journey involved writing the curriculum—the material we would teach in each session. Since then, I have gathered all of that material into one concise format—the book you are holding right now! So, I recommend this book as the primary textbook for your Journey experience. I would also recommend two other books to your participants as additional resources: *Let Justice Roll Down,* the autobiography of John Perkins, and *Bridging the Racial and Political Divide: How Godly Politics Can Transform a Nation* by Alice Patterson. These two books approach the racial divide from entirely different yet equally legitimate perspectives. (I ordered these books online and gave them to our participants at the orientation meeting, our church bearing the expense.)

Power Point presentations were used for most of the teaching sessions. I also used several video clips for illustration purposes. The dialogue questions were carefully prepared ahead of time and designed to complement each week's teaching topic. I also set up a resource table at each meeting with dozens of books and videos related to the various topics we considered. I created a list of these resources, arranged by topic, for each participant.

Meeting Topics

In order for participants to bridge the divide of race, culture, history, and politics, they must understand these issues. Therefore, teaching was a component of each meeting. As previously mentioned, the curriculum is now contained in this book, and includes six broad topics:

> **Orientation Session:** "God's New Community" (Chapter 2)
>
> **Meeting One:** "The Beauty of Diversity" (Chapter 3)
>
> **Meeting Two:** "Cultural Differences: Seeing Life through Different Lenses" (Chapter 4)

Meeting Three: "Our Shared History: Walking on Sacred Ground" (Chapter 5)

Meeting Four: "Politics: The Grand Canyon of Division" (Chapter 7) and "Righteousness and Justice: The Way of the Lord" (Chapter 8)

Meeting Five: "Present Challenges: Racial Insensitivity, Racialization and Corporate Pain" (Chapter 6)

Meeting Six: "The Culture of the New Community: Christ-centered and Spirit-empowered *Koinonia.*" (Chapter 9)

Measuring Outcomes

Because our first "Journey to *Koinonia"* was part of my doctoral dissertation project, I was required to measure and report its results. For your Journey, you may or may not choose to do this. If you do, I think you will find the results fascinating. Check out the results of our first "Journey" in Chapter 12.

Due to the highly relational nature of the Journey, I chose a "qualitative" approach to measure its results. This involved two different questionnaires, one to be administered before the Journey and the other afterwards. We used an online service called "Survey Monkey" to administer these questionnaires, sending links to the participants via email. In addition to the qualitative questions, both questionnaires asked the participants to identify their race and political ideology. Both questionnaires were completely anonymous.

The Power of Dialogue

Before closing this chapter, let me say again how essential guided dialogue is to interracial relationships. It was a vital component in our weekly meetings and contributed greatly to the positive outcomes of the Journey (see Chapter 12 for these outcomes). If you choose to lead your own Journey, I recommend that you share the following with your participants in your orientation meeting:

According to Curtiss Paul DeYoung, honest dialogue accelerates interracial relationships and leads to *koinonia*.[8] Consider the following statements about dialogue:

"We believe that every person is created in the image of God and therefore has dignity, worth, and something of value to share. So we must develop the art of listening. This will be particularly challenging as we try to listen to those whose experience in life is very different from ours. As we dialogue with people from different cultural perspectives, we will need to 'learn how to listen to voices and melodies that are unfamiliar to us.' These voices may hold the keys to unlocking the doors that open our minds to the essential components for creating our desired unity."[9]

"Dialogue is the way of community. It is the personal dimension of sharing. Dialogue concretizes the will to be in relation with another person. It is the self-conscious response of an individual with another self. It is the form of the personal; it is the way of the willed encounter, a means of grace, a celebration of shared meaning. Dialogue is the way of explored intention, the way of God who is always seeking to share himself with others."[10]

"There are bound to be differences and disagreements when people dialogue. When everyone is given a voice, a greater number of outlooks are laid out on the table. These are the moments that reveal whether our respect for the other person is genuine. For unity to be maintained, we must sincerely believe that people can disagree and still love God. One of the most damaging things in the Christian community is the spirit of judgmentalism. This spirit creeps in when one professed believer doubts

---

[8] DeYoung, *Reconciliation*, 69.

[9] Curtiss Paul DeYoung, *Coming Together in the 21st Century: The Bible's Message in an Age of Diversity*, 166.

[10] James Earl Massey, *Spiritual Disciplines* (Grand Rapids: Zondervan, 1985), 71-87. Quoted in Curtiss Paul DeYoung, *Coming Together in the 21st Century: The Bible's Message in an Age of Diversity*, 225.

the faith of another professed believer because of a difference of opinion or belief on a particular issue."[11]

Dialogue enables us to see the world through the eyes of another person. This is especially helpful when that person is from a different background—and even more so, when that person is from a persecuted community.

> "Dietrich Bonhoeffer, a German Christian martyr during the Nazi regime, developed a way of seeing the world through the eyes of others. He called this way 'the view from below.' He described it as follows: 'There remains an experience of incomparable value. We have for once learnt to see the great events of world history from below, from the perspective of the outcast, the suspects, the maltreated, the powerless, the oppressed, the reviled; in short, from the perspective of those who suffer.

> "Bonhoeffer's commitment to work for reconciliation and social justice led him to understand the importance of solidarity with the oppressed. For Bonhoeffer, solidarity was not merely living with the oppressed; it was comprehending life from the perspective of the person who suffered. The 'view from below' meant having the ability to see the world through the eyes of one who was being oppressed. Bonhoeffer allowed his life experience to mold his way of perceiving and thinking."

The Bible on Dialogue:

- "The way of a fool seems right to him, but a wise man listens … A fool shows his annoyance at once, but a prudent man overlooks an insult. … Reckless words pierce like a sword, but the tongue of the wise brings healing." Prov. 12:15-18

---

[11] Curtiss Paul DeYoung, *Coming Together in the 21st Century: The Bible's Message in an Age of Diversity,* 166).

- "My dearly loved brothers, understand this: everyone must be quick to hear, slow to speak, and slow to anger, for man's anger does not accomplish God's righteousness." James 1:19-21
- "Let your conversation be gracious and attractive so that you will have the right response for everyone." Col. 4:6

With these verses in mind, Peter Senge's definition of dialogue takes on added meaning: "Dialogue differs from the more common 'discussion,' which has its roots with 'percussion' and 'concussion,' literally, a heaving of ideas back and forth in a winner-takes-all competition."[12] True learning begins with dialogue, which is "the capacity … to suspend assumptions and enter into a genuine 'thinking together.'"[13] Reflecting on the benefit of cross-cultural dialogue, allow me to cite again a statement by Michael Pocock and Joseph Henriques:

> "When we take time to be with people, a relationship is developed. Both parties drop their masks; they respect each other's convictions and understand each other's sufferings. … As we listen to our friend's real beliefs and problems, we divest our minds of the false images we may have harbored, and we are determined also to be real. … We no longer desire to score points or win a victory. We love the person too much to boost our ego at his or her expense."[14]

On that note, Edgar Schein's concept of "talking to the campfire" proves especially helpful in interracial dialogue. This is a non-persuasive form of dialogue that avoids eye contact. Instead of looking directly at the other members of the group, the person sharing looks down at the "campfire" while speaking. Thus, the objective is not to persuade or convert others to their point of view but to open a window into their life experiences and resulting perspectives, along this line:

---

[12] Senge, *The Fifth Discipline*, 10.

[13] Ibid.

[14] Michael Pocock and Joseph Henriques, *Cultural Change and Your Church: Helping Your Church Thrive in a Diverse Society* (Grand Rapids, MI: Baker Books, 2002), 158.

"This is what I have experienced in life and that is why I see things as I do." Of course, since our meeting was held inside the church building, we didn't use a literal campfire. We set a candle on the floor in the middle of the group, and encouraged participants to look at it while speaking.

Because most of the participants had little or no previous relationship with each other, other than worshiping together on Sundays, I wanted to allow them time to develop a level of comfort with each other before launching into difficult themes. Therefore, I decided to advance the intensity of the dialogue slowly throughout the six-week Journey, beginning with milder topics in the early meetings and moving to more difficult subjects in later meetings. Remarkably, by the fourth meeting, the participants began asking if they could forego the "campfire" and talk to each other directly!

2

THE MEETINGS:
A Closer Look at Our Weekly Encounters

Following is an account of what actually took place in our meetings. Should you choose to lead your own Journey, Part Four of this book is a Facilitator's Guide that includes detailed lesson plans and information on all the materials you will see referenced in this chapter.

Orientation Session:

Prior to the official launch of our "Journey to *Koinonia*," I held an orientation session with the participants. Wanting this gathering to serve as an example of the meetings to follow, I crafted the agenda with that in mind. With the participants seated in a semi-circle, we began with prayer and a worship song. Next, we asked the participants to introduce themselves and share briefly about their faith story. A couple of techniques kept this fluid and made it fun. First, I explained that each participant had only two minutes for this exercise, and to insure compliance, I used a timer on my iPhone with a duck quack alert. Also, I handed a green Nerf ball to the first speaker, who, upon finishing his or her remarks, should toss the ball to another participant, signaling his or her opportunity to share. Only the person holding the ball was allowed to speak.

We followed this exercise with a more serious time of prayer over individual needs. After a participant shared their needs, I asked someone of the other race to anoint them with oil and lead the prayer. This was very moving and further enhanced the spiritual atmosphere of the meeting. The next activity was a time of fellowship over refreshments, followed by a teaching session. The topic was "God's New Community," the subject of Chapter 2 in this book.

I carefully explained the importance of honest dialogue as an essential component of the Journey, and I described the unique approach we would use, including the "talking to the campfire" concept. I explained the Survey Monkey pre-Journey Questionnaire that they would be asked to complete before the next meeting. I also distributed a "Memorandum of Understanding," asking each person to sign and date it. A copy of the MOU is in the Facilitator's Guide (Chapter Four of this book).

The meeting concluded with a few house-keeping matters: I distributed our "textbooks" and an article written by me titled "The Beauty of Diversity" as their reading assignment for the next meeting. (now Chapter Three in my book *Beyond Reconciliation*). I passed around sign-up forms requesting contact information and volunteers to provide worship songs and refreshments for the meetings. We also established the day, time, and location of the next six meetings. I then concluded the meeting with prayer.

As a follow-up to the meeting, I emailed each participant, thanking them for agreeing to join us on the Journey, giving them the link to the Survey Monkey pre-Journey Questionnaire, and reminding them of the day and time of our first meeting. I also prepared and sent a schedule to each participant who volunteered to lead a worship song or bring refreshments.

Meeting One:

"The Beauty of Diversity" (Chapter 3) served as the topic for the first meeting. The teaching presented diversity as God's design, both in nature and in the Church. We also explored the issue of "race" from a biblical and scientific basis, noting the difference between "race" and "ethnicity." We considered the multi-ethnic church at Antioch which replaced the mono-cultural Jerusalem Church as God's preferred model for church life.

To prepare the participants for future dialogue sessions, I distributed their answers to Question Two from the pre-Journey Questionnaire. The question read: "Do you think ethnic diversity is an accident of nature, a divine intention, or something else?" The participants thought it remarkable that their answers corresponded closely to the concepts presented in the teaching.

Meeting Two:

For worship at this meeting, we sang "Open the Eyes of My Heart, Lord," selected and led by one of the participants. The song contains the line, "Lord, I want to see you!" At the conclusion of the song, I commented that in order to truly see the Lord, we must learn to see Him through one another's eyes, with all our varied cultural perspectives. This was a fitting segue into the topic for meeting two, "Cultural Differences: Seeing Life through Different Lenses" (Chapter 4). The teaching focused on the changing demographics in America, with particular emphasis on the "six lenses of culture" that explain the ways various cultures view reality.

While the participants enjoyed food and fellowship, I arranged the chairs into a circle with a lit candle in the middle. When the participants re-gathered, I explained again the concept of dialogue as "talking to the campfire" (the candle representing the campfire). Because most of the participants had little or no previous relationship with each other (other than at worship on Sundays), I wanted to allow time to develop a level of comfort with each other before launching into difficult themes. Therefore, I decided to advance the intensity of the dialogue slowly throughout the six-week Journey, beginning with milder topics in the early meetings and moving to more difficult subjects in later meetings.

Introducing the first dialogue question ("What does it mean to you to be white/black?"), I asked them to talk about the positive rather than the painful aspects of this issue, focusing on culture rather than race. Their answers were anything but typical. For example, a white participant said, "I'm not sure exactly. White people are all mutts, you know? I'm a Scottish/Norwegian/Russian Jewish mix. White can mean so many things, really. I admire Blacks because of their cultural distinctives." A black man answered, "Our parents didn't teach us 'black' ways. I grew up around Whites. Don't look at me as black or white; get to know me as I am."

The second question, "What would you like your brothers and sisters of the other culture to know about you?" drew noteworthy responses from two black ladies. The first said, "What I would like for others to know about me: We are Americans. I am not from Africa. I am an American." The second said,

> I was born and raised in Louisiana, near the Mississippi border. How does it feel to be black? Fearful. As a child, I was told, 'Don't go to certain places. … Don't go out at night.' My biggest hang-up was my skin tone—dark. People said things to me about it, and I didn't like myself. When I grew up, I promised myself I wouldn't teach my children to be fearful. I kept them in church.

This lady then told of a distressing encounter with a white Klansman. As she shared details of this experience, the tension in the room increased dramatically, her comments advancing the dialogue further than I had intended for this meeting. However, when she concluded, I remarked, "What a great segue into our topic for next week. We're going to talk about our shared history of slavery and racism. We will look at the painful past many of our brothers and sisters share." I then asked one of the black men to pray the benediction. Before praying, he pointed to a banner on the wall that read, "And we know that all things work together for good for those who love God," and he commented, "We need to take that message home with us tonight." This proved a positive and appropriate ending for a somewhat tense moment.

Meeting Three:

Following the opening praise song and prayer, I encouraged the participants to connect for one-to-one fellowship across racial lines outside the meeting times for coffee or lunch. The teaching for this meeting, "Our Shared History: Walking Softly over Sacred Ground" (Chapter 5), focused on how Blacks and Whites see the same American history in very different ways. Describing the horrors of slavery and the humiliations of Jim Crow, I discussed the "corporate pain" that afflicts the psyche of many Blacks. To enhance the teaching, I used two video clips from the movie *Amistad.* One portrays the atrocities of the "Middle Passage." The other demonstrates how African slaves, despite harsh treatment by professing Christians, embraced the Christian gospel because of the hope it offers oppressed and suffering people. These were moving, poignant episodes. Before showing the first clip, I explained its graphic nature and asked if any would prefer not to view it. To my surprise, two black ladies left the room, commenting that they had seen the movie and would find it difficult to see it again.

Due to the intensity of the topic, we moved directly from the teaching session into dialogue. I posed Question Five from the pre-Journey Questionnaire: "What is the greatest humiliation you have ever experienced as a member of your racial group?" Their responses involved stories of discrimination and other situations in which they felt unwanted because of their race. One black man was visibly broken as he recalled being discriminated against by a government agency when he tried to open a business. Paradoxically, a young white woman tearfully shared her pain over being rejected by her black girlfriends in high school. However, she went on to recount an incident from her childhood when her grandfather disowned her family, because he saw her brother with a black girl. She told how ashamed she felt of her grandfather's racist attitude and of her race.

In this emotionally-charged moment, a black woman commented that, despite the hurt she had sustained from Whites and Blacks, she had chosen to forgive and not allow her past to define her or determine her future. I used her comment as a transition to suggest two appropriate responses to the feelings that had been shared during the meeting. For Whites who feel ashamed over the sins of their race, identificational repentance is the proper response (I explained the term and gave a biblical example). For Blacks, forgiveness is the appropriate response. For all, we should learn from the past but not allow it to define our future.

Following this meeting, my wife told me she was so moved by the dialogue, that at one point she wanted to go to every black participant and embrace them, asking their forgiveness. She suggested that we may have erred by not encouraging such expressions of repentance and forgiveness in the meeting. On the other hand, I wondered how our white participants would handle the intensity of the topic. Would they feel so ashamed and guilt-ridden that they would not want to continue the Journey? My concerns were laid to rest when a few days later I received unsolicited expressions from several white participants conveying their appreciation for this session.

Meeting Four:

This meeting involved a change in venue and format. We moved from the chapel to a large classroom with several round tables. The teaching centered on "Politics: The Grand Canyon of Division" (Chapter 6). I began with a brief video clip about abolition efforts by some of the founders in early American history. I also used a white board and flip chart to diagram the "Political Migrations of Whites and Blacks," showing how Blacks moved from Republican to Democratic ranks and white conservatives, in the opposite direction. Finally, I discussed the twin concepts of "righteousness and justice" and how together they can secure and bless any nation that adheres to them (see Chapter 8). Using a Power Point presentation, I suggested that because America was founded on principles of biblical righteousness, it ultimately achieved a measure of social justice, culminating in the civil rights movement. I also expressed the concern that many in our nation have since jettisoned some important moral foundations, exposing America to grave peril.

To launch the dialogue session, I showed a brief video clip from *Runaway Slave*. The clip features Marvin Rodgers, a black community leader calling for black Christians to "be unpredictable" to political parties. Afterwards, I added that white Christians should also "be unpredictable" to political parties. For the dialogue, the participants sat at round tables in smaller groups of four or five, both races equally represented. Dialogue questions included:

1) "Since Christians of different races often differ in their political views, is it possible for them to enjoy genuine fellowship with each other? If so, how?"

2) "Neither the Democratic Party nor the Republican Party is right or wrong all the time on every issue. Do you agree with Rodgers, that Christians—both Black and White—should 'be unpredictable' to both political parties? Why?"

3) "Do you think black and white Christians will ever join forces politically in order to marry moral righteousness to social justice? Describe some practical ways this could happen."

We appointed facilitators and asked them to keep notes on responses and report them to the whole group when we re-gathered. One participant reportedly said, "Don't discuss politics. Stop it! Don't assume what people believe. It's about Christ and love." Another participant said, "It was good to talk about these things. I believe if we are to experience genuine *koinonia,* we can't just avoid these issues and pretend they don't exist. When we truly get to know each other—our cultures and history and hearts—when we truly love each other, then we can talk openly and freely without tension." A black facilitator said that, as a result of this Journey, he will be a more informed voter and will consider the candidate, not just the party. Another facilitator said their group believes black and white Christians can come together on the issues of moral righteousness and social justice and blend our voices for positive change in America.

Meeting Five:

We used the same venue for this meeting as for meeting four, but this time, we engaged in dialogue before the teaching. After I defined a few concepts like "corporate pain," "racialization," and "racial insensitivity," participants gathered into smaller groups at round tables. Questions under consideration included:

1) "Do you think the playing field is pretty level today for a person of any race to achieve their goals and dreams?"

2) On April 27th 2013, *The Economist* magazine proclaimed on its front page, Time to Scrap Affirmative Action. How do you feel about that?"

3) "A large percentage of young black men today are incarcerated or have criminal records. Why do you think this is so?"

When we re-gathered, I asked each facilitator to share his or her group's responses to the questions. During this phase of the dialogue, having previously obtained permission, I read an email sent to me by a black participant in which he expressed his thoughts on "What It Means to Be Black." This man told about growing up in the South Carolina "Low Country" during the Jim Crow era. He shared how the trajectory of his life was positively affected during his teen years, when a white family hired him to work in their business. This family treated him like a son, even allowing him to stay in their home. This story added a positive and refreshing note to the evening and shed new light on old assumptions.

The teaching topic, "Present Challenges" (Chapter 6), dealt with persistent racial disparity in American society. I used information from Michelle Alexander's *The New Jim Crow*. To balance Alexander's approach, I cited Star Parker's *Uncle Sam's Plantation* and Dr. Ben Carson's *America the Beautiful.* The teaching also included a poignant reading from the book *Across the Divide* on the topic, "Is the Playing Field Level?"

Following the teaching, I asked the participants to join me in an exercise called "The Race," which physically demonstrates the negative effects of injustice and the unearned benefits of white privilege. The exercise began with all the participants lined up shoulder to shoulder, as if standing on the starting line of a race. As I asked a series of questions, the participants answered them by taking a step forward or backward. Once all the questions were answered, the participants were asked to observe their position relative to the other participants. This exercise clearly revealed the advantages and disadvantages associated with race in American society today.

Meeting Six:

The final meeting of the Journey involved a total change of pace. During the first hour, the participants enjoyed a steak dinner that my wife Sandra and I prepared and served as a token of appreciation for their participation. As expected, the table fellowship facilitated a wonderful time of *koinonia.*

When the meal concluded, the participants moved to the chapel where I shared an abbreviated teaching, "The Culture of the New Community" (Chapter 9). The teaching centered on the goal of the Journey—*koinonia.* I cited Paul's exhortation to the ethnically divided church at Rome to "accept one another" (Romans 15:7). In this context, the Greek word *proslambano* suggests taking someone from another culture into one's circle of friends.

An extended time of prayer seemed a fitting conclusion to the Journey. For this, we asked the participants to divide into two groups by gender. The women met with Sandra in the chapel, and the men followed me to a separate room. Gathering the men in a circle, we shared prayer needs, each man praying over his neighbor's request, until all had prayed. After the last prayer, I knelt before one of the black participants and repented for the sins I and my people had perpetrated against him and other people of color. I proceeded to wash his feet using a basin, pitcher, and towel I had prepared in advance. This man then asked if he could reciprocate my gesture, and he repented on behalf of his people for their ill-will toward Whites. This experience was well-received but not highly emotional. After further conversation, we concluded the meeting.

The women's prayer meeting went longer than the men's. Afterwards, my wife shared with me the remarkable experiences that came out of their session, which also involved repentance, forgiveness, and foot-washing. In their case, several women followed Sandra's example, spontaneously washing the feet of others while repenting and praying for them. The following sample from Sandra's account, illustrates some of what happened in the women's meeting:

> Teresa (a young black woman) stood and said tearfully, "When I saw Beverly (a young white woman) come in tonight, I knew immediately that I was to do something for her—what, I didn't know. I just knew something was wrong and she needed a touch from God. As you all know, I am very shy, and this is difficult for me, but I believe the Lord wants me to do this for you, Beverly." As Teresa washed Beverly's feet, she shared encouraging words that strengthened the bond between these two women. I confirmed to Teresa that she was ministering a "word of knowledge" about Beverly's need, because as her pastor's wife, I was aware of a situation Beverly was going through that Teresa could not have known. Afterwards, I asked everyone to stand and we concluded by singing, "We Are One in the Bond of Love."[15]

Several participants expressed sadness that the Journey had so quickly come to an end. Someone mentioned the possibility of a "Journey

---

[15] The participant names used here and elsewhere in this chapter are fictitious.

reunion" meal in the future. I sensed that a bond had developed between several of the participants over the course of the Journey.

Before concluding this final meeting, I explained the need for a post-Journey evaluation. Immediately after the meeting, I emailed the participants a link to the post-Journey Questionnaire. Although different from the pre-Journey instrument, this questionnaire was also anonymous. Happily, every participant responded, and their answers proved helpful in evaluating the benefits and shortfalls of the Journey. The next chapter offers the results of the evaluation.

3

RESULTS of the JOURNEY

It would be virtually impossible to quantify the results of an experience like the "Journey to *Koinonia*." How do you count heartaches and healing hugs? How do you measure hidden fears and falling tears or the nuances of hope as it dawns in a heart? Only God can count those things. So, I decided to use a "qualitative" approach to evaluate the results of the Journey.

The evaluation involved two questionnaires, one administered prior to the Journey and the other afterwards. The pre-Journey Questionnaire contained eleven essay-type questions asking for the participants' experiences and perceptions about various racial, cultural, and political matters. The post-Journey Questionnaire contained seven questions asking participants to evaluate the Journey, share any change in perceptions they experienced because of it, and offer advice about replicating and improving the Journey. In addition to the questionnaires, I also considered verbal and written comments from participants and observations from the actual meetings.

At the time we implemented the Journey, three goals had been uppermost in my mind:

> First, that participants begin to experience *koinonia* across racial lines—something our multi-ethnic church needed in greater measure.

Second, to foster a deeper level of understanding between the two cultures. I wanted participants to view a number of pertinent issues through each other's lenses and experience moments of insight that would enlighten and perhaps dispel previous assumptions. Thus, cross-cultural understanding was a secondary goal of the Journey.

Third, because reconciliation is a prelude to *koinonia,* I wanted participants to experience and express repentance for personal sins and to identify with the sins of their forefathers. I hoped that victims of these sins would offer forgiveness, and that some would even experience inner healing as a result.

The evidence suggests that in varying degrees, several participants realized one or more of these goals.

Goal 1: *Interracial Koinonia*

As previously stated, *koinonia* proves difficult to define in one or two English words, because it involves a spiritual component that can defy casual observation. It includes table fellowship, but it also requires a mutual experience of God's Spirit that forms a heart-to-heart bond between believers.

Reduced to its simplest expression, interracial *koinonia* evidenced itself in several aspects of the meetings: prayer and worship, fellowship over food, and verbal interaction during dialogue. Responses to Question Three on the post-Journey Questionnaire suggest that participants did experience *koinonia.* The question read, "Do you think the 'Journey' facilitated a stronger relationship between the two cultures?" Twelve participants answered in the affirmative. Here are some examples:

Black: "I can only speak for me. It helped me and I want to continue to move forward and embrace my [white] brothers and sisters."

White: "I think this group served as a catalyst to get people of different cultures to spend time together in other venues than just at church. … We have reached out to several participants to spend time together."

Black: "The concept of having us meet with someone of a different race outside of church was good, because it reinforced that we are all human and we have some differences; however, we have a lot of similarities. I think we all became more compassionate towards others."

White: "I noticed in all of our meetings that our relationships were building as they never had before. There was a 'closeness' that I had not experienced before."

A white female participant conveyed the following in an email: "I went out with Lorraine (a black participant) this past week and got better acquainted … and we have established a new … friendship. … Thank you for this opportunity. It has changed me."

Three black respondents were not as certain. One of these said, "I pray that it strengthens the relationship. … Only time will tell." Another said, "This is our hope. It is when we are challenged or … put to the test that we would really know whether or not our way of thinking has been changed." The third said, "I sense most of us already … had strong relations with the other culture. This was a great opportunity to get to know something about the person we … shake hands with on Sunday."

In response to Question Four, "As a result of this experience, will you be more likely to seek fellowship opportunities with someone of the other culture?", eleven answered, "Yes." Most added explanatory comments: "God has been speaking to me about that for a while now, and from everything I learned in this group, I know I'm on the right track. It has made my life so much more meaningful and FUN to do life with people who are different than I." Four respondents, including three Blacks, did not answer affirmatively, indicating they were already engaged in interracial fellowship, or that race would not be an issue in determining with whom they fellowship: "When an opportunity presents itself to meet someone, it does not matter to me whether you're of another race or not. … I enjoy meeting people."

Goal 2: *Cross-cultural Understanding*

The following typifies the two questions that dealt with the issue of understanding: "As a result of the 'journey,' do you feel participants of the other culture have a better understanding of your culture and/or insight into your positions?" Thirteen participants answered affirmatively. For example, a black participant commented,

> The other culture … got a chance to hear our life experiences, see the emotion and pain we endured individually and as a culture. Plus the reading material, handouts and the statistics … painted a clear picture of the devastating effects slavery and Jim Crow laws had on our people. 'The Race' … exercise we did was most effective in demonstrating the challenges our culture had to overcome to get to where we are today.

Other Blacks expressed similar sentiments:

- "Yes, I think they can now understand some of the reasons I do the things I do. I certainly understand them a lot better."
- "Definitely. Even I have a deeper understanding of my own culture."
- "I don't feel as awkward when dealing with someone of another race. They are people just like me."

By contrast, a white participant replied, "Not necessarily. I feel it was more one sided than it was mutual." This complaint has some merit. Despite my efforts to present a balanced approach, my sensitivity to black corporate pain may have cast me in the role of their advocate. Also, aware that minority people typically know more about the dominant culture than vice versa, I sought to compensate for that imbalance. At one point in the Journey, I even worried that my strong emphasis on the injustice of slavery and Jim Crow in meeting three offended white participants. After the meeting, my fears were relieved when a white participant phoned me expressing how much the meeting meant to him. He said it gave him an understanding he didn't have before and touched him deeply. About the same time, another white participant sent me a text message expressing similar feelings: "This Journey … has shaken and awakened me to the rejection the black brothers and sisters have suffered."

Other white participants expressed similar thoughts in the post-Journey Questionnaire:

- "Yes, I definitely feel that we of both cultures have a much better understanding and greater appreciation of each other. … We will be less likely to misunderstand the positions of cultures different than ourselves."
- "The dialogue helped me better understand each person's life journey and what has brought them to their beliefs and convictions."
- "We had some really great conversations where I felt comfortable being honest about my viewpoints and they seemed comfortable doing the same."
- "One thing that floored me was learning the statistics of Blacks growing up in fatherless homes and the percentage [of] Blacks … at the poverty level. … It impacted me and specifically made me more empathetic towards black men."

Goal 3: *Repentance and Reconciliation*

Certain factors suggest that some components of reconciliation, such as identificational repentance, occurred during the Journey. In the final meeting during the women's foot-washing session, an incident occurred that my wife later related to me in the following words:

Ashley (a young white woman) spontaneously knelt in front of Lindsey (an older black woman) and began to sob. She shared that about two weeks into this Journey, she learned that her great grandfather had been in the KKK. She shared her shock and grief over learning that her family had inflicted pain on people of color. Ashley then asked Lindsey to forgive her and her family. Lindsey responded, "You couldn't help it, Ashley. You had nothing to do with it. But I forgive your family for what they did."

The following comments sent by email from another white participant, reflect a similar experience:

> I am broken over the fact that I never involved myself regarding race issues, as I just felt as long as it does not affect me, I do not want to get involved. I am not a confrontational person, but a peacemaker, therefore, just did not let racial issues become my concern. That has changed during this journey. I never realized the suffering, humiliation, and rejection other non-white races suffered. I have experienced a truly broken heart now that my eyes are open to their suffering, so much so that after our meeting I went home, prayed and asked God to forgive me for my lack of concern.

Another white participant explained his empathy toward a black participant who tearfully described his "hurt and dismay" over racial discrimination: "You cannot help but feel compassion and sorrow for the wrongful actions by others."

I hoped that some of our black participants would offer forgiveness and experience inner healing as a result of the Journey. One black participant, responding to the post-Journey Questionnaire, said, "This journey was an eye opening experience as well as healing." Further evidence of reconciliation comes from some of the interactions that occurred between paricipants during the meetings, as I have cited. Here's one further example: A black participant, while telling of his experience with discrimination, had an emotional breakthrough of some kind, whether or not it involved a true "healing." After that session, he sent me an email containing the following:

> Tonight I shared my experience with racism … how a [government] inspector made passing our building inspection very difficult when [he] discovered my brother-in-law and I were black. Before tonight … I had never told anyone. I never felt the pain of that moment until [tonight]. To my surprise I got emotional telling the story. I guess what hurt the most was the fact that I lived my entire life in a multicultural world. I grew up in a small farm community of primarily white and a few black

families. We played, ate, worked and sometimes slept in the same bed. After high school I served in the Army and made friends with people of all colors and walks of life. In hindsight, I guess I could not believe a racist event had happened to me. After living [all these] years and serving over 21 years in the military I had experienced direct racism for the very first time. I thank God for not letting that one and only incident of racism cause me to develop anger or hate a person because of the color of their skin, even that building inspector. As I look back over my life I can see how God has given me the opportunity to experience the diversity HE meant for all of us.

Some white participants observed a flow of forgiveness from their black counterparts. One commented, "[The fact] that we were willing to bear some of the guilt of the past helped them to forgive us. … [It also made] it easier for them to trust us and want to embrace us as brothers and sisters." Another white participant related, "I witnessed and experienced repentance and forgiveness."

4

Journey to *Koinonia*
FACILITATOR'S GUIDE

For those who would like to undertake their own Journey to *Koinonia*, the following will guide the process. In this section, you will find weekly meeting agendas, teaching topics, dialogue questions, and handout materials.

Select the Participants: Prior to the orientation meeting, you will need to select the participants for your Journey. For the best dialogue experience, we suggest you limit the number of participants to twelve or fourteen, half of them black and half white. In your recruiting efforts, you might want to announce something like this:

> "This is your invitation to join us on a 'Journey to *Koinonia*,' a six-week, interracial small group experience. If you ever wanted to reach across the racial divide in an effort to build stronger relationships with believers from a different culture, this may be for you! In each session, we will enjoy fellowship, teaching, and guided dialogue in an effort to know and understand each other better. We will explore our differences in a respectful, spiritual, and relational atmosphere. If you are interested, join us for an orientation session that will explain the plan. The meeting will be on (date), at (time). For more information, call (contact person) at (phone number)."

Food Considerations: Each meeting of the Journey will involve light refreshments, and the participants can volunteer to provide them on a scheduled basis. The exception to this is the final meeting, which will include a full, sit-down meal. This can be a potluck supper, with the participants bringing their favorite dishes, or the church or sponsoring group might want to have it catered as a thank you to the participants.

Materials Needed for the Journey: Begin gathering the following books and DVDs which will be used in one or more of the six meetings. Publication information on each of these can be found in the bibliography at the end of this book. Since this book will serve as the "textbook" for the Journey, you will need a copy for each participant. It is available on Amazon.com or directly from the author at his email address in the publication page of this book. I recommend placing these resources on a book table for participants to browse, along with any other resources you may have on the topic. See my bibliography at the end of this book for suggestions:

Books or Booklets:

- *Beyond Reconciliation: Experiencing Koinonia across the Racial Divide* by Terry Roberts (this book) – one copy per participant
- *Let Justice Roll Down* by John Perkins
- *Bridging the Racial and Political Divide* by Alice Patterson
- *The New Jim Crow* by Michelle Alexander
- *Uncle Sam's Plantation* by Star Parker
- "Letter from Birmingham Jail" by Martin Luther King, Jr. (This can be purchased in booklet form on Amazon. It is also available in PDF format online. Secure a copy for each participant.)

DVDs:

- *Amistad* (a 1997 film directed by Steven Spielberg based on events in 1839 aboard the slave ship *La Amistad* which resulted in a heralded legal battle on behalf of the slaves.) This DVD can be purchased online.
- *The Role of Pastors and Christians in Civil Government* by David Barton. (Available at Wallbuilders.com.)
- *Setting the Record Straight: American History in Black and White* by David Barton (available from Wallbuilders.com.)

- *Runaway Slave.* This DVD can be purchased online or you can obtain the specified clip on YouTube using the following URL: https://youtu.be/6YF6XFHfsdY.

The handouts referred to in the following pages are included at the end of each meeting plan. A PDF file of all the handouts is available from the author. (You will find his email address is on the copyright page of this book).

Orientation Meeting

The Orientation Meeting is held prior to the six meetings as an opportunity to gather the participants, explain the Journey and its various components, allow them to get the "feel" of the experience, and then secure their commitment to it. It's also a great time to get the group's input on scheduling the six meetings and planning refreshments and other details.

General Preparations: The facilitator should plan and provide simple refreshments for the fellowship time at the end of the meeting. If childcare is being offered, arrange for that. Prepare the "Journey Orientation Presentation," handouts, questionnaires, etc. as needed. (All of these resources are included in this section and are available in PDF format upon request. The author's email address is on the publication page of this book.) Have copies of this book, *Beyond Reconciliation,* ready to distribute at this meeting. Consider setting up a book table with books on the topic of race relations for participants to browse.

Room arrangement: Journey meetings can be held in a home, a church classroom, or almost anywhere. Only the final meeting, which calls for separate break-out sessions for men and women, will require more than one room. For the worship, teaching, and dialogue sessions, arrange seating so that the participants are in a circle or semi-circle facing each other. Set a candle on the floor in the middle of the group. A couple of the meetings will involve a slight change in the dialogue set up, requiring three tables with chairs for participants to engage in "table talk."

<u>Agenda:</u>

- Welcome & Prayer
- Worship (The facilitator should select a praise or worship song familiar to the participants. This does not require elaborate preparation. Someone leading with a guitar or even recorded music will work fine. For the sake of time, limit this to just one song.)
- Introductions – Ask each participant to share their name and how they came to the Lord. Explain that there will be a time limit of two minutes per person, and use a timer to keep everyone on track. You will find that most people will not use the full two minutes.
- "Journey" Orientation –
    o The facilitator will give a 20 minute presentation as an orientation about the Journey (See "Journey Orientation – Facilitator's Presentation" below.)
    o Memorandum of Understanding – The facilitator distributes the MOU to each participant and walks through each point.
    o Reading Assignment – The facilitator distributes copies of *Beyond Reconciliation* (this book) to each participant and asks them to read the first three chapters before the next meeting.
    o Determine day & time of meetings
    o Send participant list around for email addresses, phone #s
    o Schedule worship songs & refreshments – Pass around a sheet for participants to volunteer to bring refreshments and to lead a worship song during the Journey.
    o Pre-Journey Questionnaire – Explain the importance of the Pre-Journey Questionnaire. Ask them to complete the questionnaire before doing their reading for the first meeting. I recommend Survey Monkey, an online service for this, which makes it simple and fun, although there is a small charge for the service. You may prefer to simply print hard copies of the Questionnaire and distribute them at the orientation meeting.
- Refreshments – Conclude the meeting by inviting the participants to enjoy some fellowship over simple refreshments.

Journey Orientation
Facilitator's Presentation

Suggestion: Create an illustrated Power Point presentation using the following points:

Purpose of the Journey:

- NOT to achieve agreement or consensus on all issues
- NOT to change each other's customs and cultural preferences
- NOT to change each other's political alignments
- TO clarify and appreciate our ethnic, cultural, and political differences
- TO foster understanding and mutual respect
- TO experience genuine *koinonia*

The Importance of Christian Unity:

- Jesus spent some of his final moments on earth praying for it (John 17:21)
- Jesus linked unity to the effectiveness of the Church's mission (John 17:23)
- Paul urges believers: "Make every effort to keep the unity of the Spirit…" (Eph 4:3)
- He says unity is both the mark and the goal of Christian maturity (Eph 4:11-13)

The Nature of Christian Unity:

- Unity does not imply uniformity
- The Antioch Church (Paul's first local church ministry) replaced the Jerusalem Church as God's preferred model for the Christian Church (Acts 11:19-24; 13:1; 1 Cor. 12:12-30)
- God delights in multi-ethnic churches!

The Nature of Koinonia:

- Often translated "fellowship" or "communion"
- A mutual sharing in the life of Jesus
- A mutual priority commitment to Jesus
- A partnership around a common Person and a common Cause
- Not hindered by diversity
- Diversity accentuates the beauty of *koinonia*
- Cannot be contained within the walls of the church building
- *Koinonia* is "doing life together"

Nevertheless, Diversity presents challenges, because of our differences. In this Journey to *Koinonia*, we will explore…

Our Differences:

- Ethnic differences
- Cultural differences
- Our shared but very different view of American History
- Different political & ideological attachments
- Different economic experiences due to the effects of "racialization"

Guiding Concerns of the Journey:

1) In light of our differing cultural and political perspectives, how do Christians in a multi-racial congregation maintain their unity?
2) Do they just overlook these differences and settle for a fragile, superficial unity?
3) Can honest dialogue foster better understanding?
4) Can Christians from diverse backgrounds accept one another without requiring consensus on social and political issues?
5) What processes will lead to biblical *koinonia* across racial and cultural lines?

Objectives of the Journey:

1) Listen to one another with respect and openness, seeking to _understand_ (not necessarily agree with) the other person's perspective
2) Acknowledge the sins of our forefathers and express "identificational repentance"
3) Understand concepts like corporate pain and racialization
4) Discern elements of racism, racial insensitivity, and resentment in our hearts and experience personal repentance

5) Receive healing for emotional wounds caused by racism and insensitivity
6) Appreciate the balance between moral righteousness and social justice
7) Learn the nature and importance of biblical unity and *koinonia*
8) Experience genuine *koinonia* across racial lines

Components of the Journey:

- Six weekly meetings consisting of fellowship, teaching, and dialogue.
- Pre-Journey and Post-Journey Questionnaires
- Extra-curricular reading and other activities
  - Personal Journaling
  - Sharing a meal, cup of coffee, or a picnic across the divide
  - Serving together in compassionate outreach

The Power of Dialogue:

"Dialogue is the way of community. It is the personal dimension of sharing. Dialogue concretizes the will to be in relation with another person. It is the self-conscious response of an individual with another self. It is the form of the personal; it is the way of the willed encounter, a means of grace, a celebration of shared meaning. Dialogue is the way of explored intention, the way of God who is always seeking to share himself with others." (James Earl Massey, *Spiritual Disciplines* (Grand Rapids: Zondervan, 1985), 71-87. Quoted in Curtiss Paul DeYoung, *Coming Together in the 21st Century: The Bible's Message in an Age of Diversity*, 225.)

"We believe that every person is created in the image of God and therefore has dignity, worth, and something of value to share. So we must develop the art of listening. This will be particularly challenging as we try to listen to those whose experience in life is very different from ours. As we dialogue with people from different cultural perspectives, we will need to 'learn how to listen to voices and melodies that are unfamiliar to us.' These voices may hold the keys to unlocking the doors that open our minds to the essential components for creating our desired unity." (Curtiss Paul DeYoung, *Coming Together in the 21st Century: The Bible's Message in an Age of Diversity*, 166.)

"There are bound to be differences and disagreements when people dialogue. When everyone is given a voice, a greater number of outlooks are laid out on the table. These are the moments that reveal whether our respect for the other person is genuine. For unity to be maintained, we must sincerely believe that people can disagree and still love God. One of the most damaging things in the Christian community is the spirit of judgmentalism. This spirit creeps in when one professed believer doubts the faith of another professed believer because of a difference of opinion or belief on a particular issue." (Curtiss Paul DeYoung, *Coming Together in the 21st Century: The Bible's Message in an Age of Diversity*, 166).

Dialogue differs from discussion, and the distinction is important. Peter Senge defines dialogue (Greek: *dia-logos*) as a "free-flowing of meaning through a group, allowing the group to discover insights not attainable individually. Dialogue differs from the more common 'discussion,' which has its roots with 'percussion' and 'concussion,' literally, a heaving of ideas back and forth in a winner-takes-all competition. Dialogue is "the capacity ... to suspend assumptions and enter into a genuine 'thinking together.'" Peter Senge, *The Fifth Discipline* (New York: Doubleday, 2006), 10.

The Bible on Dialogue:

"The way of a fool seems right to him, but a wise man listens ... A fool shows his annoyance at once, but a prudent man overlooks an insult. ... Reckless words pierce like a sword, but the tongue of the wise brings healing." Prov. 12:15-18

"My dearly loved brothers, understand this: everyone must be quick to hear, slow to speak, and slow to anger, for man's anger does not accomplish God's righteousness." James 1:19-21

"Let your conversation be gracious and attractive so that you will have the right response for everyone." Col. 4:6

"Talking to the Campfire"

"Dialogue is a form of conversation that allows the participants to relax sufficiently to begin to examine the assumptions that lie behind the thought processes." Edgar Schein recommends a low-key form of dialogue he calls "talking to the campfire," which allows participants to avoid direct eye contact. This "makes it easier to suspend reactions, disagreements, objections, and other reactions that might be triggered by face-to-face conversation." Edgar H. Schein, *Organizational Culture and Leadership*, 4th ed. (San Francisco, CA: Jossey-Bass, 2010), 391.

Such honest dialogue will not only produce a clearer understanding of differing viewpoints; more importantly, it will explain the processes behind the viewpoints—the life experiences and cultural identities that shaped them.

Dialogue Rules of Engagement:

1) Listen with openness and respect to other participants
2) Participate candidly, sharing your life experiences and true feelings
3) "Talk to the Campfire"
4) Resist the inclination to "convert" others to your viewpoint
5) Allow the Spirit of God to change your attitudes as He sees fit

Journey to *Koinonia:*
MEMORANDUM OF UNDERSTANDING

You are invited to participate in a six-week, interracial, small group learning and discovery experience called "Journey to *Koinonia*." Participants will come from diverse racial and cultural backgrounds, and hold different perspectives on a number of issues that will be considered during the "Journey." The weekly meetings will feature fellowship, learning, and dialogue. The overall objective of the experience is to foster greater understanding across racial lines and strengthen fellowship (*koinonia*) within the body of Christ.

Journey Expectations

1) attend each of the six meetings

2) complete the weekly reading assignments

3) participate candidly in the dialogue sessions, listening with openness and respect to other participants, and resisting the inclination to "convert" others to your viewpoint

4) understand that things shared during dialogue sessions should be kept confidential, that is, they are not to be repeated outside of the group meetings

5) maintain a personal journal, recording your thoughts and feelings, comfort or discomfort level, and any attitude changes you experience

6) participate in extra-curricular activities as your schedule permits (such as having coffee with a participant of the other race or serving together in ministry)

7) allow the Spirit of God to change you in any way He sees fit

Your participation is voluntary. If you choose to participate, please print your name, sign, date, and hand in to the Journey Facilitator.

____

Printed Name

_______________________________   ______________

Signature   Date

Journey to *Koinonia*
Pre-Journey Questionnaire

(The instructions below assume that printed copies of the questionnaire will be distributed at the orientation meeting. If an online service is used, such as Survey Monkey, some of these instructions will not be necessary.)

Your honest answers to the following questions will be a tremendous asset to our Journey experience. This exercise is absolutely anonymous. Not even the Facilitator will know whose answers are on the questionnaire. So please be entirely candid in your answers, and note the following guidelines:

- Use additional sheets of paper to answer the questions. Be sure to write or type the question before your answer.
- Do **not** put your name on the paper.
- After answering the questions, staple all sheets to this cover sheet, bring them to the next session, and drop them in the designated box.

1. Please select your race: Black, White, Other: _________________

2. How would you describe your political leanings: Republican, Democrat, Independent, Other, Prefer not to say: _________________

3. What does it mean to you to be White / Black?

4. Do you think ethnic diversity is an accident of nature, a divine intention, or something else? Why do you think so?

5. What would you like your brothers and sisters of the other culture to know about you?

6. How far have we progressed in the Church in addressing racial disparities and promoting reconciliation? What can our church or group do along this line?

7. What is the greatest humiliation you have ever experienced as a member of your racial group?

8. Do you think that black Christians should try to forget the past (like slavery and Jim Crow) and just live their lives in anticipation of a better future?

9. Do you think the playing field is pretty level today for a person of any race to achieve their goals and dreams?

10. On April 27th 2013, *The Economist* magazine proclaimed on its front page, "Time to scrap Affirmative Action." How do you feel about that?

11. A large percentage of young black men today are incarcerated or have criminal records. Why do you think this is so?

12. Since Christians of different races often differ in their political views, is it possible for them to enjoy genuine fellowship with each other? If so, how?

13. What are the challenges and benefits of a racially diverse church?

Meeting One
"The Beauty of Diversity"

Preparatory Sermon: If the Journey is being sponsored by a church, prior to the first meeting, it would be helpful if the Pastor would preach a sermon based on Chapter Two of this book: "God's New Community."

General Preparations: Chairs arranged in a semi-circle with candle in the middle. Arrange childcare, if being provided. Remind those who volunteered to bring refreshments or to lead a worship song. Prepare a teaching session and possible Power Point presentation from Chapter Three of *Beyond Reconciliation*, "The Beauty of Diversity."

If the Pre-Journey Questionnaire was an online survey, you should have received the responses before this meeting. Be prepared to read some of the answers to Question 4 during the dialogue session: "Do you think ethnic diversity is an accident of nature, a divine intention, or something else? Why do you think so?" (If the participants used printed Questionnaires, you can collect them as they are turned in and prepare to read some of the responses to Question 4.)

<u>Agenda:</u>

6:30 – Gather

6:35 - Opening Prayer

6:40 – Praise Song

6:45 – Teaching – *Beyond Reconciliation*, Chapter Three, "The Beauty of Diversity"

7:15 – Fellowship over Refreshments (If the fellowship time tends to run long, consider moving it to the end of future meetings, so participants can leave when they need to without missing other parts of the meeting.)

7:30 - Dialogue: In this first meeting, we are "easing" the participants into the dialogue experience by using a "safe" question that should not evoke an emotional reaction. However, before presenting the dialogue question, remind participants of the "Dialogue Rules of Engagement" shared at the Orientation meeting, perhaps using a Power Point Slide so participants can see them as well as hear them. Consider using a Nerf ball or tennis ball to indicate which participant has the floor at any given time. After stating the dialogue question, the Facilitator hands the ball to a participant, explaining that only the participant with the ball has the floor. When that participant is finished speaking, they hand the ball to another participant, and so forth.

Facilitator: "Tonight's dialogue question is taken directly from the Pre-Journey Questionnaire, and it was the topic of our teaching tonight, so you already know the 'official answer.' But, I'd like to hear your thoughts on the subject. Since this question is pretty "safe," we really wouldn't need to "talk to the campfire" tonight. However, as practice for future meetings when more difficult issues will be shared, let's give it a try (facilitator lights the candle). Here's the question: 'Do you think ethnic diversity is an accident of nature, a divine intention, or something else? Why do you think so?'" (As an aid to encourage participation, or to show that their answers were already in sync with the teaching, the facilitator can read answers from this question in the Pre-Journey Questionnaire.)

8:00 – Reading Assignment for next meeting: *Beyond Reconciliation,* Chapter 4, "Culture: Seeing Life through Different Lenses"

8:05 – Dismissal with Prayer

Meeting Two
"Culture: Seeing Life through Different Lenses"

General Preparations: Chairs arranged in a semi-circle with candle in the middle. Arrange for childcare, if being provided. Remind those who volunteered to bring refreshments or to lead a worship song. Prepare a teaching session and possible Power Point presentation from Chapter Four of *Beyond Reconciliation*, "Culture: Seeing Life through Different Lenses."

Prepare Handouts:[16]

- "Are You a Kingdom Thinker?" Pre-Test
- Poem: "The Blind Men and the Elephant"
- "Components of Ethnocentric Monoculturalism"
- "The Culture Iceberg"
- "Stereotypes – White to Black"
- "Stereotypes – Black to White"

<u>**Agenda:**</u>

6:30 – Gather

6:35 – Praise Song

6:40 - Prayer (Ask for any urgent prayer requests; ask a participant of the other race to offer prayer for the one presenting the request; if the request is for physical or emotional healing, consider anointing with oil and laying on of hands by a participant of the other race.)

6:50 – Pre-Test - Prior to tonight's teaching, distribute the handout "Are You a Kingdom Thinker" and explain that this is a personal "test" they will

---

[16] All handouts mentioned here are included in the following pages. They are also available in PDF format from the author at the email address noted on the publication page at the front of this book.

give themselves. Only they will know their answers. After they think through the questions on side one, ask them to self-evaluate their answers by reading side 2. (For confidentiality, suggest that they do this exercise mentally rather than marking the page.)

7:00 – Teaching – *Beyond Reconciliation*, Chapter Four, "Culture: Seeing Life through Different Lenses." The following handouts can be distributed during the teaching session:

- o   Poem: "The Blind Men and the Elephant"
- o   "Components of Ethnocentric Monoculturalism"
- o   "The Culture Iceberg"
- o   "Stereotypes – Black to White"
- o   "Stereotypes – White to Black"

7:25 – Refreshments and Fellowship

7:40 – Dialogue Session: Review the "Dialgoue Rules of Engagement."

Light the candle and remind participants to "talk to the campfire." Tonight's dialogue questions: (1) "What does it mean to you to be White/Black?" and (2) "What would you like your brothers and sisters of the other culture to know about you?" Discuss these one at a time. Ask participants to limit their comments to the positive aspects of their culture (customs, traditions, preferences, etc.), explaining that later in the Journey we will ask them to share some of their more painful experiences. (Use the Nerf ball if you find it helpful.)

8:15 – Reading Assignment for Meeting 3 - *Beyond Reconciliation*, Chapter Five: "Our Shared History: Walking Softly over Sacred Ground"

8:20 – Dismissal with Prayer

(See handouts for Meeting Two on the following pages.)

Are You a Kingdom Thinker?[17]

1. A family of a different culture or race moves in next door to you. You
      a. worry that property values will go down
      b. feel disappointed because you will not be able to have as good a relationship as you had with the previous neighbors
      c. get excited that you will have an opportunity to make new relationships that will stretch your world

2. When you see someone in clothing typical of another culture, you
      a. appreciate the beauty, gracefulness, creativity of the outfit
      b. wonder why they do not wear clothing more typical of your community and why are they here if they do not want to fit in
      c. resent the fact that so many foreigners live in your city

3. You notice someone speaking with an accent. You are
      a. at the grocery store
      b. at church
      c. in the "wrong" part of town

4. A large, racially different family in a late model car is stopped by the side of the road, with obvious car trouble. You
      a. think that poor people should not have so many children
      b. stop to offer assistance
      c. want to stop, but fear an encounter with people of another race

5. In a local store you see three nativity sets. In one the figures have European features and coloring, in one they have Asian features and coloring and in the third they have African features and color. You
      a. recognize that each reflects people whom Christ came to save
      b. think that two of the nativity sets are inaccurate
      c. wonder why the nativity scene you identify with isn't good enough for everyone

(Evaluate your answers on next page)

---

[17] Patty Lane, *A Beginner's Guide to Crossing Cultures: Making Friends in a Multicultural World,* (Downers Grove, IL: Intervarsity Press, 2002), Locations 2114-2156.

Evaluate your answers as follows:

If your answers were: Question 1: a, or Question 2: b, or
Question 4: c, or Question 5: c,
you may be uncomfortable with difference and what you perceive to be a
threat to your sense of security. Do you feel less secure or more threatened
when you are around people of another culture or race? Do you think this
is something that pleases God? How do you justify those feelings? Are
those justifications based on prejudice or stereotypes? What truth would
God have you learn in relation to these beliefs?

If your answers were: Question 1: b, or Question 2: c, or
Question 3: c, or Question 4: a, or Question 5: b,
you may be dealing with strong personal feelings about difference and a
tendency to pass judgment without enough information. Where do your
strong feelings come from? What experiences have shaped how you think
and feel about other cultures and races? Do those experiences give you
adequate information to make judgments regarding a culture or race? Did
Jesus in his ministry teach us anything about this kind of thinking? (For
further study read Luke 10:29-37; Mark 12:41-44; Matthew 15:21-28; John
4:4-42.) Ask God if there are any change he would like to see you make in
this area and ask for his strength to do it.

If your answers were: Question 1: c, or Question 2: a, or
Question 3: b, or Question 4: b, or Question 5: a,
you are becoming a kingdom thinker. Watch for ways God will use you in
the lives of others. Don't be surprised if he gives you opportunities to build
relationships and share your faith with people from other cultures and
backgrounds. Nurture the heart God has given you. Find ways to encourage
others in their vision for God's world. If you answered question 3 with a or
b, know that you are in a community with opportunities to form a
relationship with a person from another culture. Ask God to show you
where to begin.

The Blind Men and the Elephant

by John Godfrey Saxe (1816-1887)

It was six men of Indostan
To learning much inclined,
Who went to see the Elephant
(Though all of them were blind),
That each by observation
Might satisfy his mind.

The **First** approached the Elephant,
And happening to fall
Against his broad and sturdy side,
At once began to bawl:
"God bless me! but the Elephant
Is very like a WALL!"

The **Second**, feeling of the tusk,
Cried, "Ho, what have we here,
So very round and smooth and sharp?
To me 'tis mighty clear
This wonder of an Elephant
Is very like a SPEAR!"

The **Third** approached the animal,
And happening to take
The squirming trunk within his hands,
Thus boldly up and spake:
"I see," quoth he, "the Elephant
Is very like a SNAKE!"

The **Fourth** reached out an eager hand,
And felt about the knee
"What most this wondrous beast is like
Is mighty plain," quoth he:
"'Tis clear enough the Elephant
Is very like a TREE!"

The **Fifth**, who chanced to touch the ear,
Said: "E'en the blindest man
Can tell what this resembles most;
Deny the fact who can,
This marvel of an Elephant
Is very like a FAN!"

The **Sixth** no sooner had begun
About the beast to grope,
Than seizing on the swinging tail
That fell within his scope,
"I see," quoth he, "the Elephant
Is very like a ROPE!"

And so these men of Indostan
Disputed loud and long,
Each in his own opinion
Exceeding stiff and strong,
Though each was partly in the right,
And all were in the wrong!

Components of Ethnocentric Monoculturalism*

1. Belief in the superiority of our own culture
    a. Our history, values, language, traditions, are superior to others
    b. We are more advanced, more civilized
    c. Our way is the best way

2. Belief in the inferiority of other cultures
    a. Less developed, uncivilized
    b. Speak non-standard English, have an "accent"
    c. Seen as less intelligent and less qualified in market place and in schools

3. The Invisible Veil
    a. The imposition of the majority culture operates outside the level of conscious awareness.
    b. There is an assumption of universality: everyone shares these values
    c. Can be intentional (Neo-Nazis) or unintentional (well-intentioned individuals blissfully unaware)
    d. Unintentional complicity often the greatest obstacle to multicultural understanding

Continuum of prejudice:

1____8

Bias   Prejudice   Stereotypes   Discrimination   Bigotry   Racism   Violence   Genocide

(Everyone has some of these. Those who disavow having any biases are the ones most likely to act them out.)

*From a Lecture by Dr. Johann Mostert in a course titled, "Global & Community Leadership" (Class Notes, pp 8-9).

The Culture "Iceberg"

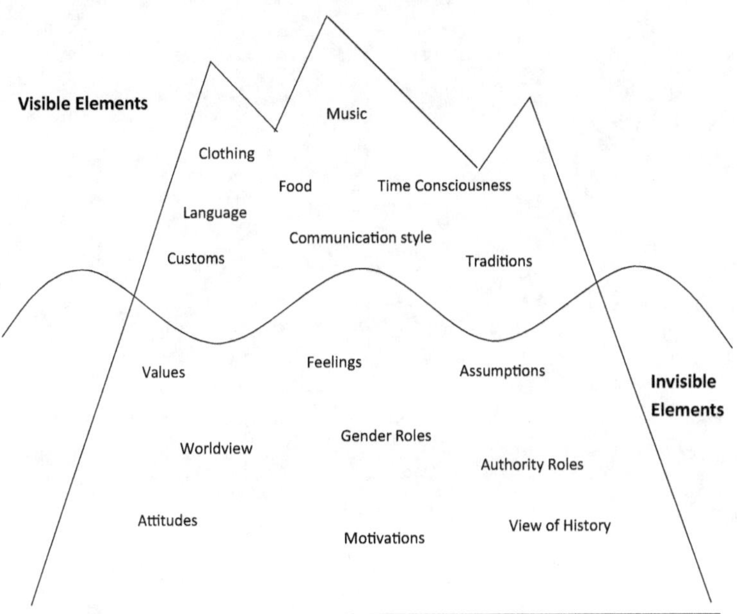

Visible & Invisible Elements of Culture

(Adapted from *A Beginner's Guide to Crossing Cultures* by Patti Lane, Location 221)

STEREOTYPES: White to Black
How We Unintentionally Reinforce Them

Each of the following statements or questions tends to reinforce negative stereotypes. See the flip side of this sheet to learn why. Before you look, give some thought as to why the statement or question might come across as offensive.

<u>10 Things Whites should not say to Blacks:</u>[18]

1. "You're not like other Blacks."

2. "You're so articulate."

3. "I actually voted for Obama."

4. "Is that your real hair?" or "Can I touch your hair?"

5. "You people."

6. "I'm color blind."

7. "Do you eat a lot of _____________?"

8. "I love your name. It's so ethnic."

9. "You don't sound Black on the phone."

10. "I don't think of you as Black."

(See next page for what's wrong with these statements.)

---

[18] Adapted from "10 Things Never to Say to a Black Coworker," DiversityInc website: www.diversityinc.com/things-not-to-say/10-things-never-to-say-to-a-black-coworker/ and "'You Must Have Voted for Obama': 5 Things Never to Say to Blacks," DiversityInc website: www.diversityinc.com/things-not-to-say/you-must-have-voted-for-obama-5-things-never-to-say-to-blacks/ Accessed February 23, 2013

What's wrong with the statements and questions on the other side:

1. One of the worst things you can say to a black person. It suggests that all others of their race are sub-standard—a very offensive stereotype.

2. On the surface, this statement appears to be a compliment, but it only reinforces the negative stereotype that in general, black people are not articulate

3. Although an attempt to create affinity or commonality, this statement comes across as superficial, provoking the response: "Don't presume to know who I support politically."

4. This question should not be asked of anyone, regardless of their race. Hair and grooming are personal. Never initiate unsolicited physical contact with anyone.

5. Referencing any demographic group as a collective "you" suggests that you intend to offend.

6. Not true. We all see color. To pretend otherwise either suggests that something is wrong with color or minimizes positive ethnic distinctions.

7. This question reveals the speaker's limited and narrow perception of black culture and cuisine.

8. This statement inappropriately accentuates racial and ethnic differences.

9. What does "Black" sound like? Again, the statement reinforces a negative stereotype about the way black people speak.

10. A backward and ignorant way of trying to compliment the person. It screams that you have a low regard for the person's ethnic group.

STEREOTYPES: Black to White
How We Unintentionally Reinforce Them

Each of the following statements tends to reinforce negative stereotypes. See the flip side of this sheet to learn why. Before you look, give some thought as to why the statement might come across as offensive.

<u>Things Blacks should not say to Whites</u>:[19]

1. "You're not diverse."

2. "There's no way you as a white person can understand."

3. "You're just a typical white person."

4. "You know you're being racist."

5. "You talk about us when we're not around."

6. "You've got all the money."

---

[19] Adapted from "9 Things Never to Say to White Colleagues," DiversityInc website: http://www.diversityinc.com/things-not-to-say/9-things-never-to-say-to-white-colleagues/ Accessed February 23, 2013

What's wrong with the statements on the other side:

1. Diversity includes white people and all people.

2. This statement may be true, but it elicits the knee-jerk response, "Then why should I even try to understand?" Don't belittle the good intentions of your white friends who simply care. Share stories from your own life journey that may open a window for them to see into your pain. Look for areas of commonality with your white friend.

3. The implication of this statement is that all white people are alike, and that all white people are predisposed to prejudice. Any language that sees white people as a group, such as 'typical white men,' is as offensive to white people as to people of color.

4. Don't assume that a comment is intentionally racist simply because it *could be* interpreted that way. Many comments are made out of ignorance to black sensibilities.

5. Being in the majority group provides freedom from the constant concern of race issues and fear of people who do not share your ethnic background. So, white people usually are *not* talking about blacks when they are not around.

6. Such a comment uses a broad generalization to make a point. Generalizations rarely open up lines of communication. A higher percentage of Blacks than Whites are poor, yet the majority of poor people are white.

Meeting Three

"Our Shared History: Walking Softly over Sacred Ground"

General Preparations: Chairs arranged in a semi-circle with candle in the middle. Arrange childcare, if being provided. Remind those who volunteered to bring refreshments or to lead a worship song. Prepare a teaching session and possible Power Point presentation from Chapter Five of *Beyond Reconciliation*, "Our Shared History: Walking Softly over Sacred Ground."

Materials Needed:

- Two clips from the DVD Movie *Amistad* (a 1997 film directed by Steven Spielberg based on events in 1839 aboard the slave ship *La Amistad* which resulted in a heralded legal battle on behalf of the slaves.) This DVD can be purchased online. The Facilitator will need to preview the movie and select the two episodes referenced in the agenda below under "Teaching."
- Article: "Bridging the Divide: Repentance and Forgiveness." Print copies for each participant.
- "Letter from Birmingham Jail" by Martin Luther King, Jr. (This is available free in PDF format online. It can also be purchased in booklet form. Secure a copy for each participant.)

<u>**Agenda:**</u>

6:30 – Gather

6:35 – Praise & Prayer

6:45 – Encourage the participants to connect for one-to-one or couple-to-couple fellowship across racial lines—have coffee, lunch, dinner, etc.—any kind of fellowship or interaction outside of our regular journey meetings.

6:50 - Teaching: *Beyond Reconciliation*, Chapter Five, "Our Shared History: Walking Softly over Sacred Ground." This teaching will focus on the tragedy of African slavery as well as the privations of sharecropping and the injustices of the Jim Crow era. To illustrate the topic of slavery, I recommend using two video clips from the movie *Amistad*. The first clip depicts the horrors of the "Middle Passage" as slaves are herded onto the ship like cattle and later, thrown overboard like a human chain. Before showing this clip, prepare the participants that what they will see is extremely graphic, and explain that if any participants would prefer not to view it, they can leave the room for the duration of this clip. The other clip demonstrates how African slaves, despite their harsh treatment, embraced the Christian gospel because of the hope it offers to oppressed and suffering people. It shows an imprisoned slave looking at the pictures of Christ in a Bible and coming to faith in Him. For the topic of "Jim Crow" and the civil rights movement, mention that each participant will receive a copy of Martin Luther King's "Letter from Birmingham Jail" for take-home reading.

7:20 – Dialogue: Review "Dialogue Rules of Engagement," reminding participants to "talk to the campfire." Dialogue Questions: Question 5 from the Pre-Journey Questionnaire: "What is the greatest humiliation you have ever experienced as a member of your racial group?" and Question 7: "Do you think that black Christians should try to forget the past (like slavery and Jim Crow) and just live their lives in anticipation of a better future?" Discuss these one at a time. (Remember the Nerf ball.)

8:00 – Refreshments and silent reading: Instead of the typical fellowship break, ask participants to serve their plates, then return to their seats to read the article "Bridging the Divide: Repentance and Forgiveness." While the participants are serving their plates, the Facilitator should place a copy of the article on each chair. After everyone has finished reading the article, encourage any dialogue that might naturally arise from it.

8:20 – Reading Assignment for Meeting Four: *Beyond Reconciliation*, Chapter Seven: "Politics: The Grand Canyon of Division"

Distribute copies of "Letter from Birmingham Jail" for take-home reading.

8:25 – Dismissal with Prayer

"Bridging the Divide: Repentance and Forgiveness"

Reconciliation is impossible without repentance. Leonard Lovett says, "The main step to the eradication of racism therefore is repentance, not just personal but collective, as in the case of white Christians."[20]

African American pastor M. L. Johnson tells of a group of white pastors in Jasper County, Texas who invited black pastors to a concert. After serving them a meal and treating them to an hour of musical entertainment, the white pastors stood together facing their black counterparts. Speaking on behalf of the white pastors, one of their number began to confess the sins of racism and injustice they and their forefathers had committed against the black community. Concluding his remarks, the speaker said, "Even though we don't deserve your forgiveness, we come before you and we ask you to forgive us." At that moment, as if on cue, the white pastors dropped to their knees. Johnson describes the moment as "a spiritual earthquake of immeasurable magnitude:"

> After about a 35 second period of silent shock, sadness, sorrow, and surprise, the sanctuary exploded under the pressure of relief from the need for repentance and forgiveness! The black audience, many silently weeping and visibly shaken, began to rise from their pews and move to the front where their white hosts were kneeling. Then they began to reach out and embrace their white brothers and sisters.[21]

"Identificational repentance," a term coined by C. Peter Wagner, means that "individuals can repent by standing in the gap as a representative for the sins of others."[22] Biblical precedents validate this concept. Daniel, Ezra, and Nehemiah identified with and repented for their fathers' sins.

Reciprocally, Blacks should freely forgive. Some argue that the living have no right to forgive on behalf of the dead. Archbishop Tutu tells the story of

---

[20] Lovett, *Kingdom Beyond Color*, locations 97–98.

[21] Johnson, *Overcoming Racism*, 370–72.

[22] Patterson, *Bridging the Racial and Political Divide*, 42.

Simon Wiesenthal, a Jew who refused to forgive a Nazi soldier's deathbed confession. Wiesenthal believed it would be presumptuous of him to do so, that it would trivialize the suffering of others. Tutu makes a compelling response to Wiesenthal. He tells of black South Africans who freely forgave on behalf of their dead and, in the process, found healing and closure for the pain of the past: "True forgiveness deals with the past, all of the past, to make the future possible. We cannot go on nursing grudges even vicariously for those who cannot speak for themselves any longer. We have to accept that [our act of forgiving is] for generations past, present, and yet to come. That is what makes a community a community."[23]

---

[23] Tutu, *No Future without Forgiveness*, 279.

Meeting Four
"Politics: The Grand Canyon of Division"

General Preparations: This week the setup is different. Have an area set up for teaching with chairs in rows facing toward a video screen and a white board. Also, set up three tables and chairs for small group "table talk." Arrange childcare, if being provided. Remind those who volunteered to bring refreshments or to lead a worship song. Prepare a teaching session and possible Power Point presentation from Chapter Seven of *Beyond Reconciliation*, "Politics: The Grand Canyon of Division."

Resources needed for this meeting:

- White Board or Flip Chart
- *Beyond Reconciliation*, Chapter Seven
- Meeting Four Dialogue Questions printed for facilitators
- Video Clip: David Barton on abolitionist movements in early American history from DVD *The Role of Pastors and Christians in Civil Government*. This DVD can be purchased from Wallbuilders.com.
- Video Clip: Marvin D. Rodgers on Black Migration from Republican to Democratic Party from DVD: *Runaway Slave*. This DVD can be purchased online or you can obtain the specified clip on YouTube using the following URL: https://youtu.be/6YF6XFHfsdY. The clip is about 5 minutes long.
- PDF Graphic: "Political Migrations"

<u>**Agenda:**</u>

6:30 – Gather

6:35 – Praise & Prayer

6:55 – Teaching - In addition to the content from Chapter Seven of this book, use the video clip of David Barton discussing abolition efforts of some of the founders in early American history. Also use the white board or flip chart to diagram the "Political Migrations of Whites and Blacks."

7:30 – Refreshments & Dialogue: Sub-divide the group into three smaller groups, proportionately black and white, and ask them to move to the three tables. Appoint a facilitator for each of the three groups, giving each facilitator a dialogue guide sheet. To save time, encourage the participants to get their refreshments, take them to the tables, and begin dialogue while they eat. Question one: "Since Christians of different races often differ in their political views, is it possible for them to enjoy genuine fellowship with each other? If so, how?"

7:50 - After they complete the dialogue for this question, have them re-assemble to watch the video clip from the DVD "Runaway Slave" and then return to their dialogue groups to consider the next question, "Do you agree that Christians—both Black and White—should be 'unpredictable' with regard to political parties? Why or why not?"

8:15 – Re-gather and ask facilitators to share one or two points that came out of the dialogue at their tables. Also make books and DVD movies on the topic available for participants to borrow.

8:20 – Reading Assignment for Meeting Five: *Beyond Reconciliation*, Chapter Six: "Present Challenges: Corporate Pain and Racialization" and Chapter Nine: "The Ethics of the New Community: Righteousness and Justice"

8:25 – Dismissal with Prayer

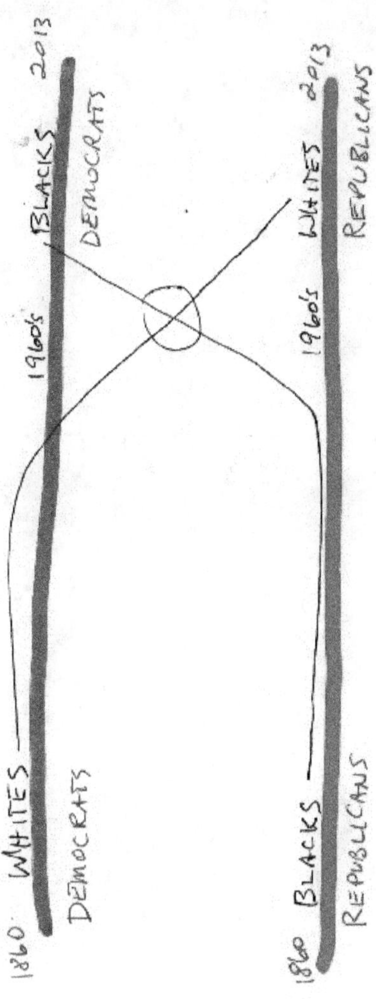

POLITICAL
THE MIGRATIONS OF BLACKS & WHITES
1860 WHITES
DEMOCRATS
1960's
BLACKS
2013
DEMOCRATS
1860 BLACKS
REPUBLICANS
1960's
WHITES
2013
REPUBLICANS

Meeting Five
"Present Challenges: Corporate Pain and Racialization"

General Preparations: This week the setup is the same as for last week. Have an area set up for teaching with chairs in rows facing toward a video screen and a white board. Also, set up three tables and chairs for small group "table talk." Arrange childcare, if being provided. Remind those who volunteered to bring refreshments or to lead a worship song. Prepare a teaching session and possible Power Point presentation from Chapter Six of *Beyond Reconciliation*, "Present Challenges: Corporate Pain and Racialization." Also, familiarize yourself with Chapter Eight: "The Ethics of the New Community: Righteousness and Justice"

Materials Needed:

- *Beyond Reconciliation*, Chapter Six: "Present Challenges: Corporate Pain and Racialization."
- Meeting Five Handout – "An Interracial Dialogue between Two Good Friends"
- "The Race"
- DVD by David Barton: *Setting the Record Straight: American History in Black and White* (available from Wallbuilders.com.)
- Excerpt from Ralph Thomas' email
- *The New Jim Crow* by Michelle Alexander
- *Uncle Sam's Plantation* by Star Parker

<u>**Agenda:**</u>

6:30 - Gather

6:35 – Praise & Prayer

6:45 – Teaching: Begin the teaching segment with a three minute video clip from the DVD *Setting the Record Straight: American History in Black and White* by David Barton. The segment deals with a few of the black heroes of the American Revolution.

Explain the concepts "Corporate Pain," "Racial Insensitivity," and "Racialization" from *Beyond Reconciliation*, Chapter Six. Briefly discuss the concept "Righteousness and Justice" as presented in Chapter Eight.

7:10 – Dialogue: Break into smaller groups again, designating a facilitator for each group. Give the facilitators a set of three questions:

> Question 1: Do you think the playing field is pretty level today for a person of any race to achieve their goals and dreams?

> Question 2: On April 27th 2013, *The Economist* magazine proclaimed on its front page, "Time to scrap Affirmative Action." How do you feel about that?

> Question 3: A large percentage of young black men today are incarcerated or have criminal records. Why do you think this is so?

7:40 – Re-gather the participants and ask each facilitator to share his or her group's responses to the questions. Allow for further dialogue.

> (During this phase of the dialogue, read Ralph Thomas' email about "What it means to be Black." Ralph's story offers a positive, refreshing contrast to the typical racism of the Deep South during Jim Crow.)

7:50 – Mention Michelle Alexander's concept known as the "New Jim Crow" and Star Parker's concept "Uncle Sam's Plantation." These are two very different perspectives by black women on the current racial situation in America. Have their books on hand as a reference for participants: Michelle Alexander's *The New Jim Crow* and Star Parker's *Uncle Sam's Plantation*. Also read from the handout, "An Interracial Dialogue between Two Good Friends."

8:20 – Explain that the final meeting will include a full meal and make arrangements for it with the participants as necessary.

8:25 – "The Race"[24] – This exercise may require rearranging the room, possibly moving tables and chairs to the perimeter of the room to allow space for the activity. Ask the participants to line up shoulder to shoulder, as if standing on the starting line of a race. As the Facilitator asks the questions, the participants are to answer each question by taking a step forward or backward (see instructions on page). Once all the questions are answered, the participants are to observe the position of their fellow participants relative to their own position. This should provide a graphic picture of white privilege and black disadvantage—the effects of racialization.

Explain the good news: "In Christ, there is no class distinction – "male or female, bond, free, Jew, Gentile – all are one." The ground is level at the foot of the cross. Also, remember Jesus' words: In the Kingdom Age, the first shall be last and the last shall be first.

8:35 – Dismissal with Prayer

---

[24] Adapted from Karen McKinney, "The Road to Understanding: A Seminar Curriculum for Unlearning Racism," paper presented in Experiential Education 694 at Mankato State University, Mankato, MN, March 1995, 22-24. Quoted in Curtiss Paul DeYoung, *Reconciliation: Our Greatest Challenge—Our Only Hope* (Valley Forge, PA: Judson Press, 1997), 92-95.

An Interracial Dialogue between Two Good Friends –
One White, the other Black

The following are excerpts from the book, *Letters Across the Divide: Two Friends Explore Racism, Friendship, and Faith,* by David Anderson and Brent Zuercher. David (black) and Brent (white) became friends in college, and later exchanged a series of letter with each other about the subject of race.

Brent (White): Have I had everything handed to me on a silver spoon because I am a white man? My ancestors were farmers who fled the Netherlands, West Prussia, and finally the Ukraine because of religious persecution. My grandparents provided for their family as best that they could. Sometimes the best included living in an abandoned railroad car and wearing clothes made out of old feed bags. My parents continued that tradition of sacrificing for the next generation and providing the best that they could. Our family was a two-income family before it became commonplace. It took the wages of both my father and mother to provide for our family of four, even though we lived rent free in a parsonage. I'm not looking for pity or sympathy, just trying to answer the question: Do you and I have equality of opportunity in this country today? I propose that we do. Our equality is the opportunity for an education, an education that gives us the necessary knowledge to obtain a job, a job that cannot be denied to either of us because of our race or gender. We have the equality to obtain the opportunity. It is what we do with the opportunities that present themselves to us that determines whether we will be successful. Does everybody start at the same point in the race? No, but that's a fact of life. Reality is that you start where the cards have been dealt and you run the race from there as best you can. When I graduated from college, I had one job offer. It was for an accounting firm I had never heard of, but they gave me a chance. (Locations 583-86)

David (Black): You see, Brent, it is easy for the advantaged to say to the disadvantaged, "Get with the program, suck it up, and be responsible." This is where sensitivity, compassion, and equality must come in. I agree that life may not have been served to you on a silver platter, but can you deny that there are advantages and preferential treatment for those who are white in this country? Are we really equal? Read the following excerpt taken from Ray Hartman's writings in The Riverfront Times regarding preferential treatment and see another perspective: Of the nation's airplane pilots, 98.3 percent are white. Of the nation's geologists, 95.9 percent are white. Of the nation's dentists, 95.6 percent are white. Of the nation's authors, 93.9 percent are white. Of the nation's lawyers, 93.8 percent are white. Of the nation's aerospace engineers, 93.8 percent are white. Of the nation's economists, 91.9 percent are white. Of the nation's architects, 90.6 percent are white. We live in a largely white country. The white majority enjoys a disproportionate share of its wealth and comfort and an even greater share of control over most of its institutions. But white power is so pervasive that it's never perceived, or even considered, white power. It's just the way things are. (Locations 609-11)

Brent: Why do whites dislike affirmative action? Why do I dislike affirmative action? I dislike any "program" that rewards people for underachievement. (locations 650-51)

David: It is very difficult for the advantaged to see the advantages they receive. As a white male, you are privileged whether you know it or not. This doesn't discount your hard work, but one day I hope you will recognize that you have the "home court" advantage. Oh, if you could only walk in my shoes for a while, my brother. If you could come play life on my court. ... Blacks are not looking for simple equality per se. Blacks are looking for justice, fairness, and the same equal access as whites. Blacks are looking for a level playing field. (locations 691-99).

Excerpt from Ralph Thomas' email:[25]

Ralph Thomas, a black participant wrote the following to clarify and expand on his answer to the pre-Journey Question: "What does it mean to you to be black?" (His name as well as other names and details have been changed to protect his privacy):

"In 1970, my freshman year in High School, two things happened that changed my life. 1st, schools were integrated without any problems. 2nd, I got a job working as a store clerk for a white family (Tom Grant) that owned a Bait and Tackle Shop. I did everything (cashiered, served customers, stocked shelves, sold ice, pumped gas and placed orders for the store); you name it, I did it. I loved the job because I got a chance to meet and develop relationships with people of all races and walks of life. The Grant family became my family away from home. I spent many nights and weekends in their home. Tom expanded his business in 1974, my last year in school. He purchased two more general stores in the South Carolina low country. He made me live-in manager of one of those stores and my best friend manager of the other. I worked for Tom until I entered service in 1976. Our friendship lasted until he and his wife died about ten years ago. In the service I found the true meaning of diversity from the beginning. My best friends were two white kids, one from England, the other from New York, a Mexican from Texas, and a guy from the Virgin Islands. I spent 21 years living with, working for and supervising people from almost every culture on earth. I really do not know what it means to be "black." Mammy and my Mom did not raise me to be "black." In the service I was judged by my character and how well I knew my job. On the battlefield, color did not matter. Thank God for putting diverse people in my life from the beginning until the present. I think I've tasted the diversity that God wants for all of us. You can see it in my family here on earth. If color was removed from what I just wrote you could not tell if I was black or white. I think God wants it that way."

---

[25] Not the individual's real name.

"THE RACE"[26]

This exercise helps individuals determine their social location. It visually demonstrates the negative effects of racialization and the benefits of "white privilege." Ask participants to stand in a line shoulder-to-shoulder, as if they were lining up for a race. Explain that they will be asked to take one step forward if they answer yes to a series of questions, and one step back if they answer yes to a second series of questions. Once all the questions are answered, the participants are asked to observe the placement of their fellow participants relative to their own position. Now imagine starting the race from their current positions. Who has the advantage?

For each question you answer with a yes, take one step forward:

1. Were there more than a dozen books in your house when you were growing up?

2. Did both of your parents graduate from high school?

3. Did you see adults reading in your home on a regular basis?

4. Did your family take regular vacations to places other than the home of relatives?

5. Did your parents own their own home?

6. Did you have a relative or friend who held a position of power in a company or the community?

7. Did you attend camp in the summer?

8. Did most of the photos you saw in schoolbooks show people of your

---

[26] Adapted from Karen McKinney, "The Road to Understanding: A Seminar Curriculum for Unlearning Racism," paper presented in Experiential Education 694 at Mankato State University, Mankato, MN, March 1995, 22-24. Quoted in DeYoung, *Reconciliation*, 92-95.

ethnic background?

9. Were most of the teachers/administrators in your school of your ethnic background?

10. Do you believe you can buy a house anywhere you want and be welcomed by your new neighbors?

11. Are you confident that, if stopped by the police, your ethnicity would <u>not</u> count against you?

For each question you answer with a yes, take one step backward:

1. Did you have a job in high school to help support your family?

2. Did you grow up in a family headed by a single female?

3. Did you have a parent who was often unemployed?

4. Did your family qualify for government assistance?

5. Did you attend college fully dependent on financial aid?

6. Was either of your parents a teenager when you were born?

7. Step back once if your skin color would be considered "yellow", twice if it would be considered "brown", and three times if it would be considered "black."

Meeting Six
"The Culture of the New Community: Christ-centered and Spirit-empowered *Koinonia*"

General Preparations: Tonight's meeting—our last in the "Journey"—will include a fellowship meal. The meal can be as simple as a potluck supper, with the participants bringing their favorite dishes or desserts. Or, the church or sponsoring group might want to have it catered as a gift to the participants—a way of thanking them for taking the risk to join the "Journey."

Obviously, the room arrangement will require tables for the meal. A second room will be needed later so men and women can move into separate meetings. The Facilitator should pre-designate someone of the opposite gender to lead the other group when the time comes for the separation of men and women.

Tonight's meeting will also involve a foot washing experience. The Facilitator should pre-select a white participant in both the men's and women's groups to initiate the foot washing by kneeling before a black participant at a designated moment. This will be further explained below.

Materials Needed:

- All items needed for the meal
- Wash basins, water pitchers, and towels for foot-washing
- *Beyond Reconciliation*, Chapter Nine: "The Culture of the New Community: Christ-centered and Spirit-empowered *Koinonia*"
- Post-Journey Questionnaire: If you are using printed versions of this, have copies ready to distribute at the end of the meeting. If you are using an online service like Survey Monkey, be prepared to email participants a link to the Questionnaire immediately after the meeting.

<u>Agenda:</u>

6:30 – Gather

6:40 – Begin Meal

7:40 – After the meal, thank everyone for their participation in the Journey. Explain about the Post-Journey Questionnaire and ask them to help us evaluate the experience by responding to the questions in a timely manner.

7:45 – Praise Song:

7:55 – Teaching: Using the content from *Beyond Reconciliation*, Chapter Nine, "The Culture of the New Community: Christ-centered and Spirit-empowered *Koinonia*," teach on the true nature of *koinonia*.

Additionally, point the participants to the section in Chapter Two titled "Accept One Another" (pages 35-37). This concerns Paul's exhortation to the ethnically divided church at Rome to "accept one another." The Greek word is *proslambano,* which means to "take someone from another culture into your life and make them a part of your circle of friends."

Finally, read the story about the "Spiritual Earthquake" that occurred in Jasper County, Texas when white pastors repented to black pastors. It's on page 115 in Chapter Six. At the conclusion of that story there is a brief teaching on "identificational repentance." Call attention to that term and explain its meaning.

8:10 – Prayer and Foot-Washing: Explain that the final part of the meeting will be an extended time of prayer for each other, men with men and women with women. Ask the men and women to move to separate areas. If the Facilitator is a male, he will need to have a designated female to lead the women's meeting. If the Facilitator is female, she will need to have a designated male to lead the men's meeting.

Explain that after a few minutes of prayer, those who so desire will have an opportunity to humble ourselves before each other by washing each other's feet, but only if they are comfortable doing so. No one should feel obligated. Begin the experience by encourage participants to share needs and pray for one another. When the moment seems appropriate, the pre-selected white participant should initiate the foot washing service by kneeling before a black participant and asking to wash their feet. While washing their feet, the white participant should engage in identificational repentance, asking forgiveness for yourself and your people for the sins committed against that person and their people. After this initial experience, the Facilitator can encourage any other participants who so desire, to follow this example. More than likely, participants of both races will want to participate without needing such prompting.

8:30 – Dismissal

Post-Journey Questionnaire

A word from the Facilitator: Thank you for joining us on the "Journey to *Koinonia.*" Please take a few minutes to evaluate the experience by answering the following questions. (Try to write a few sentences, maybe even a couple of paragraphs, for each question.) Since your answers are anonymous, please be completely candid.

Your Race

Black, White, Other: ______________________

Your Political Leanings

Republican, Democrat, Independent, Other, Prefer not to say: ______________

1. As a result of the "journey," do you feel participants of the other culture have a better understanding of your culture and/or insight into your positions?

2. Can you describe one or two things you learned about the other culture that positively changed your attitude toward them?

3. Do you think the "journey" facilitated a stronger relationship between the two cultures? In what ways?

4. As a result of this experience, will you be more likely to seek fellowship opportunities with someone of the other culture?

5. What aspect(s) of the "journey" did you enjoy the most or find most beneficial (teaching, reading materials, dialogue, fellowship, etc.)? Why?

6. Would the "journey" be a useful exercise to do again with other members of our church?

7. If we were to do the Journey again, how could we improve it?

Conclusion

Preparing this book for publication has required me to review the material you have just been reading. The emotional and spiritual experiences recorded in the accounts of the six meetings and the responses shared in the last chapter, have moved me deeply—again. In some measure, I have relived those wonderful meetings. This has whetted my appetite for more "Journey" experiences in the future. I hope it has inspired you to go on your own "Journey to *Koinonia*." If so, let me recommend my book *Beyond Reconciliation: Experiencing Koinonia Across the Racial Divide* as the curriculum companion for this guidebook. If I can assist you beyond that, feel free to contact me. My email address is on the copyright page at the front of this book.

ABOUT THE AUTHOR

For 32 years, Dr. Terrell (Terry) Roberts and his wife, Sandra, have served as the founding pastors of Trinity Church in Columbia, South Carolina. As a multi-racial congregation, Trinity Church is something of an anomaly in the heart of the Deep South. Terry is a product of the Jim Crow South, and as a young man, he accepted its racial prejudice and injustice as the norm. Fellowship with African Americans over many years opened his eyes to the beauty and power of ethnic diversity in the local church. Today, he is an advocate, not just for reconciliation, but for authentic *koinonia* (fellowship) across racial lines.

Terry holds a B.A. in Ministry from Southeastern University, a Master of Arts in Bible from Columbia International University, and a Doctor of Ministry in Church Leadership from the Assemblies of God Theological Seminary. His doctoral dissertation focused on racial relations within a multi-ethnic church.

Terry is an executive presbyter with the Assemblies of God in South Carolina and the director of their School of Ministry. Additionally, he serves on the Board of Trustees at Southeastern University in Lakeland, Florida, where he is also an adjunct professor.

Early in his life, he experienced the saving grace of Jesus Christ, resulting in a growing and fulfilling relationship with God. Today, Terry's greatest joy is sharing the message of God's love with others.

Terry and Sandra recently celebrated fifty years of marriage and ministry. They have a daughter, son-in-law, and grand-twins.

OTHER BOOKS BY TERRY ROBERTS

Beyond Reconciliation: Experiencing Koinonia Across the Racial Divide

The companion curriculum to *Journey to Koinonia*, this book explains the concept of *koinonia* and its importance to interracial relationships. It also explores in depth the differences that divide us and the bridges that bring us together across the divide.

Passing the Baton: Planning for Pastoral Transition

A concise resource for pastors and churches to help them navigate the most challenging change a congregation will ever face—pastoral transition

Five Timeless Truths: And Why They Still Matter

In this postmodern age when the concept of absolute truth has faded, there remain five enduring realities absolutely essential to life as it was meant to be lived